Andrew Green

Se

Frankenstein

Mary Shelley

Philip Allan Updates, an imprint of Hodder Education, part of Hachette Livre UK, Market Place, Deddington, Oxfordshire OX15 0SE

Orders

Bookpoint Ltd, 130 Milton Park, Abingdon, Oxfordshire, OX14 4SB
tel: 01235 827720
fax: 01235 400454
e-mail: uk.orders@bookpoint.co.uk
Lines are open 9.00 a.m.–5.00 p.m., Monday to Saturday, with a 24-hour message answering service. You can also order through the Philip Allan Updates website: www.philipallan.co.uk

ISBN 978-0-86003-766-8

Printed in Malta

Hachette Livre UK's policy is to use papers that are natural, renewable and recyclable products and made from wood grown in sustainable forests. The logging and manufacturing processes are expected to conform to the environmental regulations of the country of origin.

P01267

Contents

Introduction

Aims of the guide

The purpose of this Student Text Guide to Mary Shelley's *Frankenstein* is to enable you to organise your thoughts and responses to the novel, to deepen your understanding of its key features and aspects, and finally to help you to address the particular requirements of examination questions in order to obtain the best possible grade. Page references throughout are to the 2003 Penguin edition of the text.

It is assumed that you have read and studied the novel already under the guidance of a teacher or lecturer. This is a revision guide, not an introduction, although some of its content serves the purpose of providing initial background. It can be read in its entirety in one sitting, or it can be dipped into and used as a reference guide to specific and separate aspects of the novel.

The remainder of this Introduction section consists of exam board specifications and Assessment Objectives, which summarise in detail the requirements of the various boards and their schemes of assessment, a revision scheme which gives a suggested programme for using the material in the guide and advice on writing examination essays.

The Text Guidance section examines key aspects of the book including contexts, sources and interpretations.

The final section, Questions and Answers, includes mark schemes, model essay plans and some examples of marked work.

Exam board specifications

Frankenstein is currently on the specifications of the following examination boards:

Edexcel	English Literature AS Unit 2 (closed book examination)
OCR	English Literature AS Unit 2708 (open book examination)
AQA	English Literature AS Module 1 (open book examination)

Candidates for all boards will be set two questions on *Frankenstein* of which they must answer one. The questions will require a response to an aspect of the whole novel, or to a prescribed passage, or to an extract or extracts selected by the candidate.

Assessment Objectives

These have been set by QCA and are common to all boards. The ones relevant to this text are:

AO1	communicate clearly the knowledge, understanding and insight appropriate to literary study, using appropriate terminology and accurate and coherent written expression
AO2i	respond with knowledge and understanding to literary texts of different types and periods
AO3	show detailed understanding of the ways in which writers' choices of form, structure and language shape meanings
AO4	articulate independent opinions and judgements, informed by different interpretations of literary texts by other readers
AO5i	show understanding of the contexts in which literary texts are written and understood

This can be summarised as:

AO1	clarity of written communication
AO2	informed personal response in relation to time and genre (literary context)
AO3	the creative literary process (context of writing)
AO4	critical and interpretative response (context of reading)
AO5	evaluation of influences (cultural context)

Frankenstein has assessment weightings divided as follows:

Edexcel	Unit 2: AO1 – 5%; AO2i – 5%; AO3 – 5%; AO4 – 5%; AO5i – 10%
OCR	Unit 2708: AO1 – 10%; AO2i – 10%; AO3 – 10%; AO4 – 5%; AO5i – 5%
AQA (A)	Module 1: AO1 – 10%; AO2i – 5%; AO3 – 10%; AO4 – 5%; AO5i – 5%

Note the significantly different weighting of the Assessment Objectives between the different examining boards for the same text. It is essential that you pay close attention to the AOs, and their weighting, for the board for which you are entered. These are what the examiner will be looking for, and you must address them *directly* and *specifically*, in addition to proving general familiarity with and understanding of the text, and being able to present an argument clearly, relevantly and convincingly.

Note too that the examiners are seeking above all else evidence of an *informed personal response* to the text. A revision guide such as this can help you to understand the text and to form your own opinions, but it cannot replace your own ideas and responses as an individual reader.

Revision advice

For the examined units it is possible that either brief or more extensive revision will be necessary because the original study of the text took place some time previously. It is therefore useful to know how to go about revising and which tried and tested methods are considered the most successful for literature exams at all levels, from GCSE to degree finals. Below is a guide on how not to do it — think of reasons why not in each case.

Don't:

■ leave it until the last minute
■ assume you remember the text well enough and don't need to revise at all
■ spend hours designing a beautiful revision schedule
■ revise more than one text at the same time
■ think you don't need to revise because it is an open book exam
■ decide in advance what you think the questions will be and revise only for those
■ try to memorise particular essay plans
■ reread texts randomly and aimlessly
■ revise for longer than 2 hours in one sitting
■ miss school lessons in order to work alone at home
■ try to learn a whole ring-binder's worth of work
■ tell yourself that character and plot revision is enough
■ imagine that watching the video again is the best way to revise
■ rely on a study guide instead of the text

There are no short-cuts to effective exam revision; the only way to know a text extremely well, and to know your way around it in an exam, is to have done the necessary studying. If you use the following method, in six easy stages, for both open and closed book revision, you will not only revisit and reassess all your previous work on the text in a manageable way but will be able to distil, organise and retain your knowledge. Don't try to do it all in one go: take regular breaks for refreshment and a change of scene.

(1) Between a month and a fortnight before the exam, depending on your schedule (a simple list of stages with dates displayed in your room, not a work of art!), you will need to reread the text, this time taking stock of all the underlinings and marginal annotations as well. As you read, collect onto sheets of A4 the essential

ideas and quotations as you come across them. The acts of selecting key material and recording it as notes are natural ways of stimulating thought and aiding memory.

(2) Reread the highlighted areas and marginal annotations in your critical extracts and background handouts, and add anything useful from them to your list of notes and quotations. Then reread your previous essays and the teacher's comments. As you look back through essays written earlier in the course, you should have the pleasant sensation of realising that your writing on the text has improved. You will also discover that much of your huge file of notes is redundant or repeated, and that you have changed your mind about some beliefs, so that the distillation process is not too daunting. Selecting what is important is the way to crystallise your knowledge and understanding.

(3) During the run-up to the exam you need to do lots of practice essay plans to help you identify any gaps in your knowledge and give you practice in planning in 5–8 minutes. Past paper titles for you to plan are provided in this guide, some of which can be done as full timed essays — and marked strictly according to exam criteria — which will show whether length and timing are problematic for you. If you have not seen a copy of a real exam paper before you take your first module, ask to see a past paper so that you are familiar with the layout and rubric.

(4) About a week before the exam, reduce your two or three sides of A4 notes to a double-sided postcard of very small, dense writing. Collect a group of keywords by once again selecting and condensing, and use abbreviations for quotations (first and last word), and character and place names (initials). (For the comparison unit your postcard will need to refer to key points, themes and quotations in both texts relevant to the specific theme or genre topic.) The act of choosing and writing out the short quotations will help you to focus on the essential issues, and to recall them quickly in the exam. Make sure that your selection covers the main themes and includes examples of symbolism, style, comments on character, examples of irony, point of view or other significant aspects of the text. Previous class discussion and essay writing will have indicated which quotations are useful for almost any title; pick those which can serve more than one purpose, for instance those which reveal character and theme, and are also an example of language. In this way a minimum number of quotations can have maximum application.

(5) You now have in a compact, accessible form all the material for any possible essay title. There are only half a dozen themes relevant to a literary text so if you have covered these you should not meet with any nasty surprises when you read the exam questions. You do not need to refer to your file of paperwork again, or even to the text. For the few days before the exam, you can read through your handy postcard whenever and wherever you get the opportunity. Each time you read it, which will only take a few minutes, you are reminding yourself of all the information you will

be able to recall in the exam to adapt to the general title or to support an analysis of particular passages.

(6) A fresh, active mind works wonders, and information needs time to settle, so don't try to cram just before the exam. Relax the night before and get a good night's sleep. Then you will be able to enter the exam room with all the confidence of a well-prepared candidate.

Writing examination essays

Essay content

One of the key skills you are being asked to demonstrate at A-level is the ability to select and tailor your knowledge of the text and its background to the question set in the exam paper. In order to reach the highest levels, you need to avoid 'pre-packaged' essays which lack focus, relevance and coherence, and which simply contain everything you know about the text. Be ruthless in rejecting irrelevant material, after considering whether it can be made relevant by a change of emphasis. Aim to cover the whole question, not just part of it; your response needs to demonstrate breadth and depth, covering the full range of text elements: character, event, theme and language. Only half a dozen approaches are possible for any set text, though they may be phrased in a variety of ways, and they are likely to refer to the key themes of the text. Preparation of the text therefore involves extensive discussion and practice at manipulating these core themes so that there should be no surprises in the exam. An apparently new angle is more likely to be something familiar presented in an unfamiliar way and you should not panic or reject the choice of question because you think you know nothing about it.

Exam titles are open-ended in the sense that there is not an obvious right answer, and you would therefore be unwise to give a dismissive, extreme or entirely one-sided response. The question would not have been set if the answer were not debatable. An ability and willingness to see both sides is an Assessment Objective and shows independence of judgement as a reader. Do not be afraid to explore the issues and do not try to tie the text into one neat interpretation. If there is ambiguity it is likely to be deliberate on the part of the author and must be discussed; literary texts are complex and often paradoxical, and it would be a misreading of them to suggest that there is only one possible interpretation. You are not expected, however, to argue equally strongly or extensively for both sides of an argument, since personal opinion is an important factor. It is advisable to deal with the alternative view at the beginning of your response, and then construct your own view as the main part of the essay. This makes it less likely that you will appear to cancel out your own line of argument.

Choosing the right question

The first skill you must show when presented with the exam paper is the ability to choose the better, for you, of the two questions on your text where there is a choice. This is not to say you should always go for the same type of essay (whole-text or passage-based) and if the question is not one which you feel happy with for any reason, you should seriously consider the other, even if it is not the type you normally prefer. It is unlikely but possible that a question contains a word you are not sure you know the meaning of, in which case it would be safer to choose the other one.

Do not be tempted to choose a question because of its similarity to one you have already done. Freshness and thinking on the spot usually produce a better result than attempted recall of a previous essay which may have received only a mediocre mark in the first place. The exam question is unlikely to have exactly the same focus and your response may seem 'off centre' as a result, as well as stale and perfunctory in expression. Essay questions fall into the following categories: close section analysis and relation to whole text; characterisation; setting and atmosphere; structure and effectiveness; genre; language and style; themes and issues. Remember, however, that themes are relevant to all essays and that analysis, not just description, is always required.

Once you have decided which exam question to attempt, follow the procedure below for whole-text and passage-based, open- and closed-book essays.

(1) Underline all the key words in the question and note how many parts the question has.

(2) Plan your answer, using aspects of the key words and parts of the question as sub-headings, in addition to themes. Aim for 10–12 ideas. Check that the Assessment Objectives are covered.

(3) Support your argument by selecting the best examples of characters, events, imagery and quotations to prove your points. Remove ideas for which you can find no evidence.

(4) Structure your answer by grouping and numbering your points in a logical progression. Identify the best general point to keep for the conclusion.

(5) Introduce your essay with a short paragraph setting the context and defining the key words in the question as broadly, but relevantly, as possible.

(6) Write the rest of the essay, following your structured plan but adding extra material if it occurs to you. Paragraph your writing and consider expression, especially sentence structure and vocabulary choices, as you write. Signal changes in the direction of your argument with paragraph openers such as 'Furthermore' and

'However'. Use plenty of short, integrated quotations and use the words of the text rather than your own where possible. Use technical terms appropriately, and write concisely and precisely, avoiding vagueness and ambiguity.

(7) Your conclusion should sound conclusive and make it clear that you have answered the question. It should be an overview of the question and the text, not a repetition or a summary of points already made.

(8) Cross out your plan with a neat diagonal line.

(9) Check your essay for content, style, clarity and accuracy. With neat crossings-out, correct errors of fact, spelling, grammar and punctuation. Improve expression if possible, and remove any repetition and irrelevance. Add clarification and missing evidence, if necessary, using omission marks or asterisks. Even at this stage, good new material can be added.

There is no such thing as a perfect or model essay; flawed essays can gain full marks. There is always something more which could have been said, and examiners realise that students have limitations when writing under pressure in timed conditions. You are not penalised for what you didn't say in comparison to some idealised concept of the answer, but rewarded for the knowledge and understanding you have shown. It is not as difficult as you may think to do well, provided that you are familiar with the text and have sufficient essay-writing experience. If you follow the above process and **underline**, **plan**, **support**, **structure**, **write** and **check**, you can't go far wrong.

Text Guidance

Frankenstein

Contexts

Assessment Objective 5 requires candidates to 'evaluate the significance of cultural, historical and other contextual influences on literary texts'. There are a number of significant contexts within which the reader needs to place *Frankenstein*, all of which provide illuminating information when approaching the text.

Historical context

Mary Shelley: key dates and works

1797	30 August, Mary Godwin is born to William Godwin and Mary Wollstonecraft; mother dies 10 days later.
1812	Percy Bysshe Shelley pays regular visits to Godwin and meets Mary.
1814	Mary begins a relationship with the married Shelley.
1815	Gives birth to a daughter, who dies shortly afterwards.
1816	Gives birth to a son; moves to Geneva; Shelley's wife drowns; he marries Mary.
1817	*Frankenstein* completed.
1818	*Frankenstein* published.
1819	Semi-autobiographical novel *Mathilda* written.
1822	Percy Bysshe Shelley dies, lost at sea.
1823	*Valperga* published.
1824	Mary publishes her husband's *Posthumous Poems*.
1826	*The Last Man* published.
1830	*Perkin Warbeck* published.
1836	William Godwin dies.
1837	*Falkner* published.
1844	*Rambles in Germany and Italy* published.
1851	1 February, dies in London.

About the novel

The idea for Mary Shelley's most celebrated novel famously came during a summer stay with her husband, Percy Bysshe Shelley, and Lord Byron on the shores of Lake Geneva in Switzerland, very near to Victor Frankenstein's home town of Geneva. In the course of the visit, at Lord Byron's suggestion, a ghost story-telling competition occupied the company and as a result Shelley was inspired to begin her tale. *Frankenstein*, or *The Modern Prometheus*, was first published anonymously in 1818 in three-volume form, when Shelley was only 20 years old; a two-volume edition, bearing the author's name, came out in 1823, and a revised single-volume publication was printed in 1831. Deeply concerned with social issues, individual and social morality, and the question of humanity, the novel unmistakably bears the imprint of Shelley's parents, Mary Wollstonecraft and William Godwin. Wollstonecraft is recognised as one of the great early champions of female rights and as a progenitor of the feminist movement, producing such central writings as *Maria* and *A Vindication of the Rights of Women*, whilst Godwin was famed both as a novelist (*The Adventures of Caleb Williams*, *Mandeville* and *Fleetwood*) and as a political thinker, whose treatise *Enquiry Concerning the Principles of Political Justice* was profoundly influential. In addition, the work draws heavily on the influence of the Romantics (especially Wordsworth, Coleridge and Shelley), and Milton's great poetic masterpiece *Paradise Lost*. Central in their significance too are the works of the Gothic canon; Shelley's journal makes explicit the extent to which she was dependent on the classic works of Gothic fiction — she had read the works of Ann Radcliffe, Matthew Lewis (who visited the party on the shores of Lake Geneva), Charles Maturin and William Beckford, all central figures in the establishment of the Gothic form.

Gothic context

Whilst many critics have tended to see the Gothic as a loosely defined form, it is nevertheless possible to identify a wide range of features typical of works that fall within the genre. The following list covers the most common, all of which are highly significant in a consideration of *Frankenstein*:

- wild landscapes (mountains, sea, ice caps in *Frankenstein*)
- ruined or grotesque buildings (typically castles, granges, houses, mansions; in *Frankenstein*, however, charnel houses, the garret in Ingolstadt and the hovel in Scotland are central)
- religious settings/religious concepts (churches, abbeys, monasteries, convents)
- sensibility (the cult of emotion) and sudden shifts of emotion
- excess and extremity (location, emotion, violence, cruelty, perversion)
- the supernatural and ghostly (the monster in *Frankenstein*) — also figurative 'ghosts' of the past or the future which haunt the characters
- imagery of darkness, shadow, decay
- the exotic and oriental (the role of Safie)
- horror and terror
- isolation and loneliness (relating to both setting and character, including orphaning, widowing)
- blurring of distinctions between sanity and insanity
- sex and sexuality, including obvious sexual overtones of the frequently used towers (phallus) and caverns (vagina)
- use of multiple narrators
- crime, lawlessness and abuse

- absolute power — often tyrannical and including abuse
- stock characters (absent mother, wicked father/father-figure, helpless heroine, the villain (often linked to religion), hopeless lover, the criminal)
- the devilish and arcane
- use of the historical past (interestingly absent from *Frankenstein*, although the novel does present the 'histories' of the central characters)
- the outsider

These devices are employed extensively by Mary Shelley; however, *Frankenstein* cannot be seen as conventionally Gothic in the sense that the works of Ann Radcliffe or Matthew Lewis are, as any comparison with these authors will make clear. Equally, however, Shelley relies to a significant extent upon the stock tools of the Gothic genre. You need to be prepared and able to consider the use and subversion of Gothic convention within the novel.

Roots and manifestations of the Gothic

The Gothic first emerged as a recognisable form in the mid- to late-eighteenth century. *The Recess* (Sophia Lee), *The Old English Baron* (Clara Reeve) and *The Castle of Otranto* (Horace Walpole) all date from this period and are generally recognised as the first flourishing of the form. It was with the works of Ann Radcliffe (*The Mysteries of Udolpho*, *The Romance of the Forest* and *The Italian*) and Matthew 'Monk' Lewis (*The Monk*) that the classic nature of the form and a fuller critical definition of it began to be established. These two authors may be taken to represent the two contradictory impulses in the Gothic between literature of terror and literature of horror. The form continued to develop and flourish in the work of authors such as Charles Maturin (*Melmoth the Wanderer*), James Hogg (*The Private Memoirs and Confessions of a Justified Sinner*), William Godwin (*Caleb Williams*) and his daughter Mary Shelley, whose greatest novel is *Frankenstein*.

In the Victorian era Gothic continued to develop in the work of Sheridan le Fanu (*Uncle Silas*, *The Wyvern Mystery*) and in the tales of Elizabeth Gaskell, among others. A new direction was established, however, through the sensation novels of authors such as Wilkie Collins and Mary Elizabeth Braddon. Towards the end of the nineteenth century and into the twentieth, new versions of the form continued to proliferate in the decadence of Wilde (*The Picture of Dorian Gray*), Stevenson (*Dr Jekyll and Mr Hyde*) and Stoker (*Dracula*), the ghost stories of Henry James, M. R. James and Sir Arthur Conan Doyle, and the great adventure novels of Doyle, Haggard and H. G. Wells. In all of these writers, where fear of the outsider in the closing years of Empire is paramount, the way is paved for the more overtly arcane and horrific that has tended to dominate the form over the last century.

Roots

The roots of the Gothic, however, precede the work of Walpole, Lee and Reeve. The following list suggests a number of the key authors and movements which influenced the rise of the Gothic form:

- Elizabethan and Jacobean tragedy (supernatural, vice, corruption, imprisonment, brutality, sexuality)
- graveyard poetry (Blair, Young, Parnell; focus on decay and death)
- William Blake (the dimension of the religious; the essential coexistence of opposites)
- the Romantics (notably Wordsworth, Coleridge and de Quincey; focus on the natural world and its relation to the state of mankind)
- the Novel of Sensibility (with its excess of emotion and extremity)
- Milton (the dimension of religion; the battle between good and evil)
- medieval Gothic (the focus on the grotesque)

Manifestations

There are inevitable difficulties in attempting to define any genre. This difficulty is multiplied in relation to the Gothic, in that the form has taken on so many different manifestations. In addition, there are many sub-groups, such as some branches of science fiction, the western, the thriller and the detective novel, which frequently make use of the techniques of Gothic whilst never fully engaging with it. Below is a broad outline of the various mainstream forms:

- romance (Ann Radcliffe, Charlotte Dacre, Clara Reeve)
- sensation (Wilkie Collins, Mary Elizabeth Braddon)
- mystery/adventure (Sir Arthur Conan Doyle, Henry Rider Haggard, H. G. Wells)
- fantasy (H. G. Wells, J. R. R. Tolkien, Mervyn Peake)
- ghost story (Henry James, M. R. James, Sir Arthur Conan Doyle, Susan Hill)
- horror (Edgar Allan Poe, James Herbert, Stephen King)
- arcane (H. P. Lovecraft)
- decadence (Robert Louis Stevenson, Oscar Wilde, H. G. Wells, Bram Stoker, Arthur Machen)

Although the authors identified cover an enormous range of styles and concerns and a considerable range of time, any consideration of their work against the typical elements of the Gothic will make clear their links.

The reading list at the end of this guide provides plentiful additional and comparative reading material, enabling you to undertake a structured course of private reading to extend your response to the novel through comparison with a range of other texts. This will help to develop your awareness of the typical elements of the Gothic form in its various manifestations, and to consider how they inform one another.

Dualisms within the Gothic

The Gothic is a form that thrives on the fruitful recognition of opposition and division. As has repeatedly been observed by critics, it is a genre that abides on the borders and extremes of experience, and as such the stark use of opposition is both appropriate and unavoidable. The very nature of the genre depends upon uncertainty and the possibility of violent shifts. The unsettling and the indefinable have a central role to play in any Gothic novel, and *Frankenstein* is no exception. If the reader is to be disturbed and uncertain about the true nature of what he/she sees, the deployment of uncertainty through opposites is essential. Uncertainty is of particular importance in *Frankenstein*, as the novel deals with questions of moral, social, religious and personal doubt. This is true of Gothic fiction, poetry and drama in general, where the recognition of opposition and uncertainty is one of the key areas of concern. The appearance of these issues within the Gothic genre is frequently allied to political and social concerns, often reflected in periods of social, religious and moral unrest.

Below is a list of a number of the most commonly used oppositions and divisions within the genre:

- good/evil
- innocence/guilt
- Catholic/Protestant
- freedom/imprisonment
- pursued/pursuer
- natural/unnatural
- terror/horror
- moral/immoral/amoral
- light/dark
- male/female
- reality/fantasy
- natural/supernatural
- human/inhuman
- internal/external
- high/low (mountains/abysses)
- large/small
- the defined/the undefined
- living/dead/(undead)

The impact of such oppositions and their use in the Gothic novel is profoundly unsettling for the reader. This is certainly significant in considering the author's intentions. Victor Frankenstein faces a sequence of momentous social, religious, ethical and personal choices, all of which may be summed up in pairs of opposites. Shelley's presentation of these issues is never straightforward, and the reader's response cannot be straightforward either. The ambiguity the reader feels in relation to the central issues of the novel leads to a deep ambivalence in his/her attitude towards Frankenstein and the monster. At one and the same time, the reader is aware that the monster and his creator are part of the same 'being', but are polar opposites too. As such, they may be seen to embody the essentially contradictory nature of the Gothic genre.

Gothic images

Many artists have worked in what may be termed a Gothic style. William Blake and Goya are two of the best known examples, alongside the French artist, Gustave Doré. Blake was both a poet and an artist, producing a sequence of books which were a synthesis of art and words; he considered that the two were inseparable in his art, and as such an informed 'reading' of his pictures is essential to an understanding of his work. A number of his literary works adopt the typical Gothic device of working through opposites, such as *The Songs of Innocence and Experience* and *The Marriage of Heaven and Hell*. He also produced images for such evocatively named poems as *The Grave* by Robert Blair and *The Complaint, or, Night-thoughts on life, Death and Immortality* by Edward Young. Goya is another highly significant figure, referred to by Davenport-Hines as 'the greatest painter to have had gothic moods'. He also recognised this propensity in himself when he wrote: 'Fantasy abandoned by reason produces impossible monsters.'

In approaching a Gothic text such as *Frankenstein*, it is essential to be aware not only of the literary but also of the artistic context of writing. You will find an exploration of some examples of Gothic art both an enlightening and a fascinating exercise. Mary Shelley, along with other great Gothic authors, such as Edgar Allan Poe, Charles Maturin, Ann Radcliffe and Matthew 'Monk' Lewis, depends to a great extent on the visual impact of her words. As you read, take time to visualise the scenes she 'paints' for you.

It would be interesting and informative for you to spend some time looking at some or all of the following pictures, all of which are easily available on the internet:

- Goya: *The Sleep of Reason Produces Monsters* (*El Sueño de la Razon Produce Monstruos*) — Richard Davenport-Hines (1998) refers to this painting as 'Perhaps the most important single image for the historian of the gothic.'
- William Blake: *Good and Evil Angels*
- Henry Fuseli: *The Nightmare*
- Caspar David Friedrich: *The Cross in the Mountains*

When you look at these paintings, try to identify the typical themes and concerns of the Gothic which are identified later in this guide. Look closely at a range of these images and use them as the basis of a series of short reflections, outlining the ways in which these paintings can illuminate our understanding of the Gothic form.

Below are two of the images Gustave Doré produced to illustrate Coleridge's poem 'The Rime of the Ancient Mariner'. This poem was one of the most significant literary influences on *Frankenstein*. A comparison of the settings and atmosphere of these images and the setting of the frame narrative of the novel provides the reader with a clear sense of the impact Coleridge's poem made upon the young Mary Shelley.

The importance of the poem to Mary Shelley and her novel may be illustrated by the following anecdote. When she was a girl, Coleridge visited the Godwin household. In the evening, Mary and her siblings reportedly hid behind the sofa to hear the great poet recite his most famous work. Mrs Godwin, Mary's stepmother, threatened to send them off to bed. Coleridge, however, intervened, pleading that they be allowed to stay and listen, thus paving the way for one of the greatest of all tales of Gothic horror.

Mary Evans Picture Library

Luigi Galvani

One of the most important influences on Shelley in her writing of the novel came from the world of science. Working at the University of Bologna in the 1780s, Luigi Galvani performed a series of experiments involving electric charges and frogs. He discovered that an electric charge applied to the spinal cord of a frog could generate muscular spasms, even if the legs were no longer attached to the living frog. He became convinced he was seeing the effects of what he called 'animal electricity'.

In one strange case, the effect was achieved when the frog's legs were in no direct contact with a source of electricity. Galvani wrote:

> While one of those who were assisting me touched lightly, and by chance, the point of his scalpel to the internal crural nerves of the frog, suddenly all the muscles of its limbs were seen to be so contracted that they seemed to have fallen into tonic convulsions.

Luigi Galvani, performing one of his experiments

Mary Evans Picture Library

In a further extract from an account of his experiments he wrote:

> Therefore having noticed that frog preparations which hung by copper hooks from the iron railings surrounding a balcony of our house contracted not only during thunder storms but also in fine weather, I decided to determine whether or not these contractions were due to the action of atmospheric electricity…. Finally…I began to scrape and press the hook fastened to the backbone against the iron railing to see whether by such a procedure contractions might be excited, and whether instead of an alteration in the condition of the atmospheric electricity some other changes might be effective. I then noticed frequent contractions, none of which depended on variations in the weather.

Galvani's remarkable experiments established a basis for the study of neuro-physiology and neurology, and established the electrical nature of nerve-muscle function. His name lives on in the term 'galvanism'.

The direct relevance of this to *Frankenstein* is clear. Galvani, as a scientific researcher within the field of the natural sciences, is immediately established as a counterpart to Frankenstein, obsessed with the determination to prove his theories. The links are closer than this, however. The novel's focus upon the concept of vivifying and animating dead matter comes directly from the experiments of Galvani, and in both the novel and Galvani's work the presence of atmospheric electricity and lightning storms is significant. The grotesquerie of Frankenstein's experimentation and its place in our cultural, popular and literary heritage clearly owes much to the figure of Galvani.

Geographical context

Mapping the novel

The settings of Frankenstein are scattered across Europe. The map below shows where the events take place. (Note: the North Pole is not shown.)

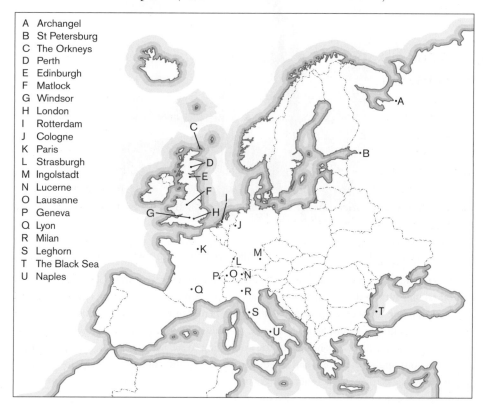

A Archangel
B St Petersburg
C The Orkneys
D Perth
E Edinburgh
F Matlock
G Windsor
H London
I Rotterdam
J Cologne
K Paris
L Strasburgh
M Ingolstadt
N Lucerne
O Lausanne
P Geneva
Q Lyon
R Milan
S Leghorn
T The Black Sea
U Naples

Shelley makes use of a diverse range of settings. This serves to emphasise the rootlessness of the lives of both Frankenstein and his creature. It is a symptom of the excess and extremity that is such a characteristic of the novel, and demonstrates the impossibility of escape for both Frankenstein and the monster; they live in a world increasingly desolate and void of other significant human interest. It also suggests the universal nature of the danger Frankenstein has unleashed on the world.

Locations of events in the novel

- Russia: St Petersburg, Archangel, Black Sea
- Arctic circle
- North Pole
- Switzerland: Lucerne, Geneva, Jura mountains, Belrive, Lausanne, Mont Salève, Chamounix

- Italy: Naples, Como, Milan, Leghorn
- Germany: Ingolstadt, the de Laceys' cottage, Strasburgh, Rhine Valley, Cologne
- France: Paris, Lyon, Rhône Valley
- England: London, Windsor, Matlock, the Lake District
- Holland: Rotterdam
- Scotland: Perth, Edinburgh, the Orkneys
- Ireland

Topography and location

Initial bearings

From the very outset, *Frankenstein* is heavily dependent upon notions of travel and place. In the introductory letters of Robert Walton and the first chapter of Frankenstein's narrative alone, the reader is taken on a journey from London to St Petersburg; to Archangel on the White Sea and the ice floes of the Arctic Ocean; then south to Geneva and Lucerne in Switzerland, Milan and the Italian Lakes, as well as Germany and France, providing the reader with a stunning array of physical landscapes. It is thus quickly established that both travel and location are to be central in the unfolding of Shelley's tale.

Shelley's purposes in bombarding the reader with the geographical are pivotal to understanding the novel and its impact. Not only do the locations provide us with a panoramic view of early-nineteenth-century Europe and beyond; they also link closely to the novel's greater concerns. The powerful questions of ethics and the permissible boundaries of scientific research, the tormented psychology of Victor Frankenstein, and the tortured existence of the monster he creates, considerations which sit at the very heart of this great novel, are all intimately bound up in the use Shelley makes of her wide-ranging choices of location and the notion of the journey or travel.

To the ends of the Earth

The novel begins with Robert Walton, whose letters and brief concluding narrative frame the central narrative of Frankenstein himself. As both a man of science and an explorer, Walton embodies for us the connection between travel, location and the great themes of the text which have already been identified. For the same reasons, he also mirrors the character of Frankenstein. This is a connection which Shelley is quick to establish. Walton, in want of a friend with whom to share his interests, identifies in Frankenstein, soon after he has saved him from the ice, 'a man who, before his spirit had been broken by misery, I should have been happy to have possessed as the brother of my heart' (p. 28).

Likewise, Frankenstein observes the affinity that exists between them. He sees in Walton something of his own fatal propensity: both men are victims of the same flaw — the inability to place responsible bounds on their quest for knowledge.

Walton's incapacity 'to be persuaded that the pole is the seat of frost and desolation' (p. 15) is alarmingly similar to Frankenstein's unwillingness to heed the warnings of Clerval and Elizabeth. His determination to acquire knowledge whatever the cost and wherever it may lead has already set him on the same fateful quest.

It is wholly fitting, therefore, that Walton's journey, which is just beginning, should be interrupted by Frankenstein's, which has now become one of never-ending pursuit; the pursuit no longer of knowledge, but of the inescapable and poisoned fruits of it. Their fortuitous meeting as the ice surrounds Walton's ship, threatening it with destruction at every minute, encapsulates the entirety of Frankenstein's strange and harrowing story. The ice encircling the ship becomes the embodiment of Frankenstein's mad obsession, the encroaching danger that faces Walton if he should not heed the tale he is about to hear.

The concept of the journey as embodying the quest for knowledge is clearly a central device within Shelley's narrative, but equally important, as has already been suggested, is where the journey leads to. For this reason it is entirely appropriate, indeed necessary, that the novel should open and close at what was then, and still largely remains, one of the great undiscovered frontiers, and that so much of its disturbing action should take place in locations characterised by their wildness. The reader is presented not simply with untamed Gothic landscapes, but with locations which embody the very nature of the parable Shelley tells. Place has an integral part to play in the operation of her tale. As Frankenstein himself is aware, the extreme nature of the story we are offered depends upon the willingness of the listener to operate at the utmost limits of experience and plausibility, an extremity which has to be embodied in the settings. '"Were we among the tamer scenes of nature,"' he observes to Walton, '"I might fear to encounter your unbelief, perhaps your ridicule; but many things will appear possible in these wild and mysterious regions."'

There is, then, a clearly stated intention behind Shelley's use of location. In dealing with the extremities of human nature and in considering the lengths to which human beings will allow themselves to be pushed by their unquenchable desire for knowledge, the use of untamed locations is central. The landscapes she presents the reader with become a metaphor for the rugged harshness and uncon-trollable wildness to which single-minded, irresponsible determination can lead. They become the fearsome frontiers of human intellect.

The mountains of the mind

It is not the intellect alone, however, that is significant when considering Shelley's employment of location and the journey. The concerns of the text go beyond the purely intellectual, approaching the psychological, and this, too, is reflected in the use she makes of these concepts. From the outset of the novel, the reader is aware of the fact that Walton and Frankenstein are more than common men. Walton states that 'there is a love for the marvellous, a belief in the marvellous, intertwined in all my projects, which hurries me out of the common pathways of men, even to the wild sea and unvisited regions I am about to explore'. When he goes on to identify in the eyes of Frankenstein 'an expression of wildness, and even madness', the reader becomes aware of the masterful way in which Shelley uses the physical, the extremity of her landscapes to build up the psychological profile of her characters.

The icy wilderness of the pole, which Walton is approaching, and where Frankenstein is found, can be seen as a powerful image of the psychology of the two men. As it is a physical wilderness, a place of threat, death and destruction, so it can be seen to represent the spiritual wilderness that is Frankenstein's reality and Walton's inheritance if he should fail to learn from his warning and continue with his journey. The drifting ice floes which threaten Walton's expedition from the start and which encroach upon the ship, bringing him into contact with Frankenstein, are a symbol of spiritual and moral entrapment. Walton, less advanced on the path towards destruction, is able to escape their clutches, but Frankenstein, faced with the ineradicable need to confront and destroy the product of his own obsession, is obliged, at the end of the novel, to return to the ice, the spiritual wasteland which he has made his own destiny. He is left to drift away into the freezing seas which are the extremities of human morality and psychology.

The disturbing impact of Shelley's warning is heightened by the contrast she makes of conventional nature alongside the wild locations already identified, an antithesis as disconcerting for the reader as it is for the protagonists. Frankenstein, fated because of his own actions to live a life haunted by extremity in the wilds of the world, remains nonetheless keenly aware of the beauty of the natural world around him. 'Even broken in spirit as he is,' Walton informs us, 'no one can feel more deeply than he does the beauties of nature. The starry sky, the sea, and every sight afforded by these wonderful regions, seems still to have the power of elevating his soul from earth'. It is part of Frankenstein's torture that the nature he would so love still to enjoy has become his torment. Indeed, as if to point out the hideous irony of his dilemma, it is from nature that he draws the metaphor for his downfall: 'when I would account to myself for the birth of that passion, which afterwards ruled my destiny, I find it arise, like a mountain river, from ignoble and almost forgotten sources; but, swelling as it proceeded, it became the torrent which, in its course, has swept away all my hopes and joys.' Not content to accept and enjoy the wonders of nature, Frankenstein has allowed the thirst for knowledge and understanding to develop into a self-destructive passion.

Isolation

This brings us to the very heart of the matter. Frankenstein, relating his terrible tale to Walton, has arrived at the realisation of the dire straits into which his journey has led him, and where it will inevitably continue to lead. His future, as so much of his past, is to be a place of isolation. Through his arcane research he has one by one cut the ties with his family and friends until he stands alone with his hope — the dream of a perfect companionship with his creation; a dream which leads to the nightmare of his dreadful fate.

Once more a comparison with Walton is instructive. As the Captain is setting out on his journey towards what he perceives as the magnificent promises of the polar regions, he laments his lack of a companion 'who would have sense enough not to despise me as romantic, and affection enough for me to endeavour to regulate my mind'. He recognises the need to avoid the unchecked isolation which could lead him into the 'madness' that he knows he is capable of, and which he is later to see embodied by Frankenstein. He identifies within himself the potential monster his quest for knowledge may conjure up, the monster which he has already seen in the distance as he stands on the deck of his ship; a monster which, as the central narrative of the novel makes clear, is itself tragically fated to a life of rejection and isolation from humanity, banished like its creator to the wildernesses of the world.

The journey of the narrative

The significance of the opening and closing sequences of the novel, which deal with the coincidence of the journeys of Walton, Frankenstein and the monster at the wildest frontiers of nature and knowledge, cannot be overestimated. It at once focuses the attention of the reader upon the central concerns of location and journey which, as we have seen, play such a significant role within the course of the novel. It should come as no surprise, therefore, to note by way of conclusion the structural 'journey' that Shelley employs within the text.

The outer narrative of Walton encloses that of Frankenstein, which in its turn encloses that of the monster. The narrative is itself a journey which begins where it must end; a circular form, emphasising the destructive futility that is one of the novel's central themes. The narratives of Walton, Frankenstein and the monster can thus be seen as one narrative; their journeys as one and the same journey. The three beings are modifications of one being — they are mankind and the question of its future. The novel is a journey to and through the very heart of our species, a place full, Shelley suggests, of potential, whether for good or for evil.

Literary contexts

Paradise Lost

John Milton's epic poem, first published in 1667, is of central importance to a reading of *Frankenstein*. As one of the books read by the monster, it is a formative influence on his view of the world, but it is also a formative influence on the narrative as a whole. What follows is a brief synopsis of the plot, designed to help you think about the parallels between the poem and the novel.

Paradise Lost is based on the biblical story of Adam and Eve, taken from the book of Genesis. It tells of how they were created and, through an act of disobedience to God, find themselves banished from the Garden of Eden, or Paradise. The poem also tells the story of Satan, originally known as Lucifer, an angel who leads an attempted rebellion against God, and who is punished by being sent to hell. As an act of revenge against God, he causes the Fall of mankind by tempting Eve in the form of the serpent.

Synopsis

Book 1 — in hell, Satan and his followers, recovering from their defeat in an attempted rebellion against God, build a palace called Pandaemonium (a word Milton coined himself).

Book 2 — they debate the possibility of returning to battle, but decide instead to investigate a new world God is creating, 'another World, the happy seat/Of some new Race call'd Man', where they may be able to exact a safer form of revenge.

Book 3 — Satan goes to the new world alone. Sin and Death, his offspring, allow him out of hell and he undertakes a perilous journey through Chaos. He disguises himself as 'a stripling Cherube' and tricks the angel Uriel into showing him the way to the dwelling place of Man.

Book 4 — once on the earth Satan resolves 'Evil be thou my Good' and finds his way to the Garden of Eden. He manages to gain entrance to the garden, where he finds Adam and Eve living in idyllic perfection and grows jealous of them. He learns that they have been given only one prohibition by God — that they must not eat the fruit of the Tree of the Knowledge of Good and Evil. Gabriel and the other angels, warned by Uriel, capture Satan and throw him out of Paradise.

Book 5 — Eve relates to Adam the tempting dream Satan has inspired. The angel Raphael warns Adam and Eve about Satan, God's enemy. He tells them they are privileged beings, designed by God one day to replace the fallen angels in heaven.

Book 6 — Raphael recounts Michael and Gabriel's battle with Satan.

Book 7 — Raphael tells of God's decision to create another world and describes the six days of creation, ending with a renewed warning about eating the fruit of the Tree of Knowledge.

Book 8 — Adam relates his memories of his own creation and his plea to his maker for a companion. Raphael departs with a warning about the relationship between the sexes.

Book 9 — Satan, not to be so easily deterred, returns to earth and enters the body of a serpent. He finds Eve alone, and tricks her into eating the fruit of the forbidden tree. Adam, when he learns of this, resigns himself to his fate and also eats the fruit. They immediately lose their innocence, and become aware of their nakedness.

They fall into despair, aware that in disobeying God (rebelling as Satan has done) they have separated themselves from him. Satan has gained his revenge on God by spoiling the best thing he has created.

Book 10 — God sends his son to judge his sinful creation. Evil-doing has now entered the world, and Sin and Death build a highway from hell to their new home, the earth. Adam and Eve recognise what they have done and resolve to seek mercy from the Son of God.

Book 11 — seeing their penitence, the Son of God intercedes for Adam and Eve, but God decrees that they must leave Paradise and sends the angel Michael to banish Adam and Eve. Michael outlines the effects of original sin in the murder of Abel and the subsequent miseries of humankind, ending with the flood.

Book 12 — Michael tells in outline the rest of the history of the Old Testament, revealing to Adam and Eve a hope for the future in the figure of a coming Saviour. Adam and Eve leave the Garden of Eden in sadness, but resolved on obedience and submission.

Interestingly, the poem has been substantially illustrated on a number of occasions. William Blake, whose paintings draw considerably on the Gothic tradition in the visual arts and whose poetry is full of Gothic excess, illustrated the poem in 1806. Gustave Doré, who provided a set of illustrations for Coleridge's 'The Rime of the Ancient Mariner', also illustrated *Paradise Lost* in 1866. This further strengthens the connections in the mind of the reader between the main source texts of *Frankenstein*. Remember too that *Paradise Lost* is given a specifically formative role in the life and perceptions of the monster, who finds and reads a copy of the poem.

Characters

Throughout *Frankenstein* Shelley makes extensive use of Milton's great poem, using Milton's main characters to represent or parallel the situations of her own main characters.

One of the most striking aspects of *Frankenstein* is Shelley's deliberate division or sharing of the characteristics of Milton's main characters. Both Frankenstein and the monster take on elements of each of the following:

Adam

The monster

Like Adam, the monster is Frankenstein's first creation. Faced with the prospect of a life spent alone, again like Adam, he is isolated, unfulfilled and needs a companion, which he requests from his creator. As events progress, he knowingly commits acts of sin against his creator. As Adam did, the monster enters the world with a mature body, but with an 'unformed' mind, which has to make sense of a totally new world. Like Adam, the monster is banished from 'Eden'; in the case of the monster, however, the 'Eden' in question is the possibility of a loving and meaningful relationship with his creator.

There are also two striking ways in which the monster and Milton's Adam are seen to contrast. Given the many ways in which they compare, these two areas of contrast are all the more arresting. Unlike Adam, the monster is never allowed the pleasure of a partner, as his companion is destroyed. The other significant difference is that, unlike for Adam and Eve, there is no promise of a coming saviour to give the monster a hope for the future. These two key areas of contrast mark the monster as a tragic figure, destined for destruction.

Frankenstein

Frankenstein, like the monster and Adam, commits an act of sin against his creator, God. The cost of this is that he is banished from a happy relationship with his creator and the natural world which gives him so much pleasure and delight. There are many ways in which Frankenstein's relationship with his family, a luxury afforded to neither Adam nor the monster, may be seen as a paradise; this paradise he loses irrevocably as a result of his 'sin' in metaphorically eating the forbidden fruit of knowledge. In his loss of Elizabeth he may also be said to lose another 'paradise'. According to Milton and his biblical source, the consequence of eating the fruit of the forbidden tree was death. This was not immediate death, but as a consequence of their actions in eating the fruit, mortality entered the world; it is as a result of Frankenstein's 'forbidden' experimentation that death enters the novel, embodied in the monster.

God

The monster

Like God, the monster holds power of life and death over Frankenstein. He also consistently sits in judgement over him. As he reminds Frankenstein: 'I am your master.' As the God of the Old Testament is described as a jealous God, pursuing vengeance against the sinful, even down the generations, so the monster becomes a vengeful, god-like figure watching over the movements of Frankenstein with almost omniscient powers. The result is that, like God, he forces Frankenstein out of the 'paradise' of his family and marriage.

Frankenstein

Frankenstein plays God in his experimentation in anatomy and his eventual creation of the monster. However, unlike God, who places his creation in the wonderful surroundings of the Garden of Eden, Frankenstein at no point displays any caring sentiments towards his creation. He forces the monster from the 'paradise' of society, but unlike God, this is for no good reason: the monster's 'original sin' is his ugliness, not a defect in his personality. Like God, Frankenstein is requested by his creation to provide a companion, which he begins to do, but he does not complete this; his creative impulses are turned into destructive desires.

Satan

The monster

As Satan does (and similarly, Adam and Eve), the monster rebels against his creator. It is worth noting, however, that unlike Satan, Adam and Eve (and his own creator, Frankenstein), he does not do so without good cause. Once he has decided upon rebellion, like Satan he seeks to exact revenge on his creator by attacking the thing he loves most; Satan attacks the newly created humans that God so loves and the monster attacks Frankenstein's family and loved ones.

The monster, like Satan, is capable of enduring amazing hardship. Satan undertakes his daring and phenomenal journey across Chaos, and the monster lives under the harshest of conditions and repeatedly travels through and in spite of great danger. Satan is ejected from heaven by God because of his rebellion, and similarly the monster is thrown out of the heaven of social relations by his creator, Frankenstein.

A further similarity between the monster and Satan is their strange attraction for the reader. Neither can be seen as a conventional villain. William Blake's famous observation that Milton was 'of the devil's party without knowing it' is an observation that could equally be applied to Shelley's view of her monster. The feelings of the reader towards the monster are frequently feelings of sympathy and pity. In his decision to pursue a course of evil instead of good (he later comments that '"Evil thenceforth became my good"') he echoes almost exactly Satan's resolution: 'Evil be thou my Good.'

Frankenstein

In his forbidden pursuit of the ability to create life, Frankenstein puts himself in the place of God, effectively pitting himself against his creator. This is very similar to Satan's rebellion, when he and his legions seek to displace God in heaven. Such attempts at the usurpation of the divine position and the divine right place both Frankenstein and Satan in direct opposition to God, an opposition for which they must pay the penalty. The consequence of rebellion against God is separation and ejection from heaven. This impacts upon Frankenstein in two ways: first he is separated from God in that he loses the ability to pray — such prayers as he does offer are prayers of vengeance, hellish prayers of destruction. In this separation he gradually falls into despair, a despair represented in part by his increasingly tainted relationship with the beauty of the natural world — a symbol of Eden. Second, in a strange reversal of roles, he finds himself banished from the 'heaven' of his family by his master, the monster. Frankenstein recognises the similarities between himself and Satan, observing: '"like the archangel who aspired to omnipotence, I am chained in an eternal hell."'

In summary

The use Shelley makes of God, Adam and Satan to represent both the monster and Frankenstein adds to the reader's growing sense that Frankenstein and the monster may be one and the same. Applying a Freudian emphasis on the divided self, such a reading becomes not only distinctly possible, but also profoundly necessary in understanding the full impact of the relationship between Frankenstein and the monster. As God created man in his own image ('Then God said, "Let us make man in our image, in our likeness"', Genesis 1:26), so Frankenstein creates the monster to be a perfected version of himself. The man created by God is to be a reflection of his nature, and similarly the monster must be seen as integral to the nature of Frankenstein himself.

The parallels of the monster and Frankenstein to Adam and God respectively also create another impact on the reader. They identify forcefully the extent to which Frankenstein fails in his duty towards his creation. God, in spite of the rebellion of the man and his companion, continues to love them and is genuinely pained by their actions and the ruin of his creation; so much is shown by his decision to send his son as the saviour of humanity alluded to in both the Bible and Milton's poem. Frankenstein, however, demonstrates no such love. His paternal, even god-like dreams before the creation of the monster fade instantly when he sees the fruits of his work. The emotions he feels are not like God's, the emotions of genuine grief and love, but rather the selfish outcome of disappointed hope.

Both Frankenstein and the monster are like God in that they wield power, though, unlike God, neither wields it wisely. The monster, however, maintains to the last a sense of the respect he owes to Frankenstein as his creator, whilst Frankenstein only fleetingly entertains the responsibilities due from himself as creator towards his creature.

Satan as a figure of energetic vengefulness and determination reflects on the reader's perception of both Frankenstein and the monster. Both the monster and Frankenstein find themselves animated and consumed by the passions of revenge.

Other characters

It is not only the two central characters of the text that link to the poem. Elizabeth, Frankenstein Senior and Clerval also draw characteristics and plot roles from the poem. As in *Paradise Lost*, a group of angels (Uriel, Raphael and Michael) attempts to protect the innocence of Adam and Eve, so the immediate friends and family of Victor seek to protect him from the encroaching dangers that face him and from which he is clearly incapable of protecting himself. Frankenstein Senior, for example, warns his son to avoid the '"sad trash"' to be found in the works of Paracelsus and Albertus Magnus. Clerval nurses his friend back to health when he falls ill after the creation of the monster and also accompanies him, almost like a guardian angel, on his trip to England. Elizabeth, as the 'heavenly' language which Frankenstein repeatedly applies to her would suggest, is similarly cast in the role of angel. She compares to Eve, as the companion of Frankenstein, although significantly she is not the cause of her partner's temptation.

Language of heaven and hell

The Gothic, as has already been established, is a genre that makes considerable use of opposites and contrasts. The ultimate contrast, in terms of the Christian tradition within which the novel operates, is the contrast between heaven, the perfection of union with God, and hell, the eternal torment of separation from God. Shelley makes much use of the language of heaven and hell in the course of the novel. This clearly links to the Bible, but also connects significantly with Milton's poem. Note particularly the extent of Frankenstein's language of hell and things hellish in reference to the monster, who is repeatedly referred to as 'the fiend' and as 'diabolical'. Almost as a compensation within Frankenstein's view of the world, he uses an equal build-up of language of the heavenly in the context of his mother and Elizabeth who represent for him (in terms of their femininity, their caring natures, their love and their beauty) everything that he will not allow the monster to be.

Examples

(1)   'But I will not be tempted to set myself in opposition to thee. I am thy creature, and I will
       be even mild and docile to my natural lord and king, if thou wilt also perform thy part, the
       which thou owest me.' (pp. 102–03)

Here the monster introduces the relationship between creature and creator in terms that bring to mind the relationship between God and Adam, or God and humanity. The respect that the monster vows to accord Frankenstein, if he will do what he should, is the same respect that Frankenstein should be showing to God. Frankenstein has not been either 'mild' or 'docile', but has set himself up in opposition to God — like Satan in Milton's poem.

The monster, speaking of the hovel he inhabited next to the de Lacey's cottage, observes that: '"it presented to me then as exquisite and divine a retreat as Pandaemonium appeared to the daemons of hell after their sufferings in the lake of fire"' (p. 108). Compare this to *Paradise Lost* I, ll.670 ff, where Milton writes of the building of Pandaemonium as a refuge from the horrors of Hell.

(2) The monster comments in detail on the influence Milton's poem has had upon him, the complex interrelations between creature and creator, and his view of himself:

'But *Paradise Lost* excited different and far deeper emotions.... I often referred the several
situations, as their similarity struck me, to my own. Like Adam, I was apparently united
by no link to any other being in existence; but his state was far different from mine in every
other respect. He had come forth from the hands of God a perfect creature, happy and
prosperous, guarded by the especial care of his Creator; he was allowed to converse with
and acquire knowledge from beings of a superior nature: but I was wretched, helpless, and
alone. Many times I considered Satan as the fitter emblem of my condition; for often, like
him, when I viewed the bliss of my protectors, the bitter gall of envy rose within me...no
Eve soothed my sorrows nor shared my thoughts; I was alone. I remembered Adam's

supplication to his Creator. But where was mine? He had abandoned me, and in the bitterness of my heart I cursed him.' (pp. 132–34)

(3) Frankenstein observes:

...some softened feelings stole into my heart, and dared to whisper paradisiacal dreams of love and joy; but the apple was already eaten, and the angel's arm bared to drive me from all hope. (p. 193)

The specific reference to Adam and Eve's sin demonstrates that the fate of Frankenstein and the monster has already been sealed; there is no way back into paradise from the point they have reached.

'The Rime of the Ancient Mariner'

Samuel Taylor Coleridge's great poem, published in 1798 in *Lyrical Ballads*, is another text that influenced Mary Shelley profoundly in the composition of *Frankenstein*. Detailed comparisons in terms of plot material, concepts, location and imagery can all be found within the poem, and a full and close reading of the poem is therefore to be recommended.

Synopsis

Part 1 — a wedding guest, just about to go in to the wedding banquet, is stopped by a strange old man who mesmerises him into listening to his tale. He tells of a sea voyage. The ship is driven south by a severe sea-storm into the Antarctic regions, where its safety is threatened by encroaching ice. One day the ship is approached by an albatross (birds sailors believe to be inhabited by the souls of dead sailors). The ice breaks and the ship is released. The albatross follows it. In fear, the mariner recounts how he (inexplicably) killed the bird.

Part 2 — the other sailors believe he has done 'an hellish thing' to kill the albatross. The wind dies and they find themselves becalmed in the southern ocean. Isolated and in danger, the ship is surrounded by strange creatures from the deep and a number of supernatural visitations take place. The sailors hang the body of the albatross around the mariner's neck by way of punishment for his deed. The mariner finds himself isolated and detested by the rest of the crew.

Part 3 — still becalmed, the ship is approached by another boat, which is strangely able to move despite the lack of wind and tide. It is crewed by a lone woman and her companion, Death. The boat pulls up alongside, but then disappears at great speed and darkness falls instantly. One by one the sailors die in rapid succession, leaving the mariner alone on the ship.

Part 4 — the wedding guest fears that he is talking to a ghost, but his fears are allayed by the mariner, who continues his tale. Surrounded by the corpses of the sailors, which oddly do not rot, and bizarre sea creatures, the mariner tries to pray but cannot. For a week he remains unable to pray, but at last, when he finds himself so desperate for companionship that he is able to thank God even for the company of the sea creatures, the albatross falls from his neck and sinks into the sea.

Part 5 — rain and a violent wind spring up and the ship, strangely protected from the wind, begins to move. The dead sailors bizarrely rise to crew the ship. The mariner believes their bodies have been inhabited by good spirits. 'Moved onward from beneath', the ship makes good progress away from the polar region. Suddenly it stops and the mariner, falling into a trance, hears voices in the air announcing that he has more penance to do.

Part 6 — the mariner wakes from his trance to find the 'ghostly crew' all staring at him. Another wind rises and pushes the ship back to its home port. It stops in the harbour. The ghostly crew members fall to the deck and an angel appears to stand on each corpse. Attracted by the strange lights in the bay, the ship is approached by the harbour pilot and a hermit.

Part 7 — as they pull alongside, a fearful rumbling begins; the waters of the bay split open and the ship sinks, leaving only the mariner afloat. He is rescued by the pilot. The mariner tells his tale to the hermit. This will not suffice, however, and periodically he is overcome by a powerful compulsion to tell his tale again. The wedding guest returns to the feast 'a sadder and wiser man' for hearing the mariner's tale.

Direct links

> I am going to unexplored regions to 'the land of mist and snow'; but I shall kill no albatross, therefore do not be alarmed for my safety, or if I should come back to you as worn and woeful as the 'Ancient Mariner'. You will smile at my allusion; but I will disclose a secret. I have often attributed my attachment to, my passionate enthusiasm for, the dangerous mysteries of ocean, to that production of the most imaginative of modern poets. (pp. 21–22)

These words of Captain Walton's at the very outset of the novel immediately establish the importance of Coleridge's poem and its function in the novel; in the mind of the reader Walton's reference is to take on a significance and symbolic weight that will belie the apparently humorous and light-hearted allusion. To the alert reader the seeds of danger are already sown: Walton's attachment to Coleridge's poem has already created in him a passionate desire for the dangers of the ocean, a place where he will soon be forced to face the very dangers the Ancient Mariner himself faced and where he will meet, in Victor Frankenstein, a man tormented by an 'albatross' of his own. Shelley clearly wishes the reader to be in no doubt from the very outset that the events of this poem are highly significant and the reader needs to be alert at all times to the allusions Shelley makes to the poem.

Some of these allusions are at the level of plot whilst others are symbolic. The visit of the mariner to the polar regions, for example, clearly parallels the Artic journeys undertaken by Walton and Frankenstein. Likewise, both texts depend to a large extent on the ghostly and supernatural, and make considerable use of the all-important albatross. Extreme locations and the natural world are used in the poem and the novel to reflect the extremity of the situations faced by their respective protagonists. The Ancient Mariner and Frankenstein are the tellers of cautionary tales that they find themselves compelled to relate for both cathartic and altruistic reasons. They have both committed thoughtless actions that haunt them for the rest of their lives, forcing them to live in isolation from their fellow men. As Frankenstein observes (p. 60), quoting directly from Coleridge's poem and comparing himself explicitly to the Ancient Mariner, he is:

> Like one, on a lonesome road who,
> Doth walk in fear and dread,
> And, having once turned round, walks on,
> And turns no more his head;
> Because he knows a frightful fiend
> Doth close behind him tread.

When the reader thinks about how this stanza links specifically to the plot, vocabulary and ideas of Shelley's novel, a number of highly significant connections emerge. Isolation, fear and dread are shared by Frankenstein and the Ancient Mariner; they are central concerns of Shelley's novel and of the Gothic genre in general, dealing with the darker areas of the human psyche. The fateful progression implied in this stanza is also significant; the sense of the inescapable and the indefinable are central to the power of Shelley's work, making Frankenstein a truly tragic figure. The endless travel and torment Coleridge invokes here is also a vital aspect of *Frankenstein*; the concept of the journey, whether physical, spiritual or psychological, is at the very heart of both works, and Shelley's allusions to the poem import a whole world of meaning, fear and supernatural despair into the novel. Coleridge's invocation of the stalking, frightful fiend is highly suggestive, echoing Frankenstein's perpetual sense of fear and the reader's certainty that he is forever watched by the vigilant monster. Such effects are augmented by the vocabulary of the devilish which informs poem and novel alike.

The albatross

Like the Ancient Mariner with his albatross, Frankenstein is cursed to carry about with him the burden of what he has done. He refers to his promise to create a companion for the monster as 'this deadly weight yet hanging round my neck, and bowing me to the ground' (p. 157). Then, later in the novel he observes: 'I was cursed by some devil, and carried about with me my eternal hell' (p. 207). These two observations and the overt allusions they make to the condition of the Ancient Mariner are highly significant for the reader. The symbolic importance of the albatross in Coleridge's poem is transposed onto the situation of Frankenstein in the course of the novel: the monster, his promise to create a companion for the monster, his fascination with science, the heavy weight of death for which he is responsible, the fear of what will happen to the members of his family and a growing feeling of guilt and isolation are all 'albatrosses' around Frankenstein's neck.

Other characters in the novel suffer from the same kind of burdens: Elizabeth Lavenza and Frankenstein's father suffer from Frankenstein's absence (abandonment); Justine Moritz suffers the burden of false accusation; the monster suffers because of his ugliness and isolation; Walton's love of exploration is a threatening weight around his neck.

Locations

A detailed consideration of the locations used by Coleridge and Shelley is vital. Both poem and novel make highly effective use of the polar regions. They do this primarily to achieve their effects of eerie strangeness: the barrenness and harshness of the physical location with its unrelieved whiteness, brilliant displays of light, the 'endless' summer days of the bizarre midnight sun, and the impenetrable winter nights, add considerably to the reader's sense of otherness and danger. In both texts these regions are the home of bizarre creatures and the supernatural. The concept of isolation is also central within *Frankenstein*; like the Ancient Mariner, for the monster, Frankenstein and Captain Walton the pole is the place of utmost isolation from their fellow men. In this, the location reflects one of the most significant themes of Shelley's novel, where isolation within human existence appears to be the norm rather than the exception. As a place of extremity — it is literally the end of the earth — the pole offers a peculiarly appropriate location for the extreme events we witness and a striking contrast to the more 'civilised' environs of the Ancient Mariner's England and Frankenstein's Switzerland; the hostile and potentially deadly environment takes on the symbolic power of the coldness and darkness associated with the place. Finally, the pole is the place of nemesis, where the Ancient Mariner, Frankenstein, Captain Walton and the monster (and the reader) are forced to come face to face with their destinies and the horrible reality of the consequences of their actions.

The Prometheus myth

Along with 'The Rime of the Ancient Mariner' and *Paradise Lost*, the Prometheus myth is a central source text for *Frankenstein*, which bears the subtitle *The Modern Prometheus*. Prometheus, whose name means 'forethought', is a divine being, one of the Titans descended from the union of the Sky God with the Earth Mother. In some stories he appears as the creator of the human race, but is always their champion. When humans were denied fire by Zeus, Prometheus stole it for them from heaven. His punishment, retold by Mary Shelley's husband Percy Bysshe Shelley in his poem *Prometheus Unbound*, was to be fastened to a cliff in the

Caucasus where an eagle daily tore at his liver which grew back again each night to be torn again the next day.

Shelley's use of the Prometheus myth within her novel is deeply ironic. 'Forethought' certainly does not apply to the actions and ideas of Frankenstein. His lack of forethought or any rational thought at all in relation to the monster he creates is striking. Similarly, the comparison of Frankenstein with a divine being, the champion of humankind, is also blackly comic.

Viewed from another perspective, however, Shelley's use of the myth adds weight to her moral tale. The novel tells of Frankenstein's spiritual and moral journey, the implications of which are given still greater significance and resonance through the parallels that Shelley invokes with her mythological source. From the reader's perspective, the tale of Prometheus, who created mankind, bears clear relation to that of Frankenstein, the creator of the monster. Similarly, Prometheus's punishment for stealing the fire of the gods significantly connects to Frankenstein's fate after he disowns his creation. Sentenced by Zeus to be chained forever to a rock in the wilderness of Mount Caucasus, Prometheus's liver is perpetually eaten out, just as Frankenstein is forever destined to pursue the monster through the wilds of the earth, and to be destructively torn apart by remorse at the outcomes of his arrogant research.

The comparison is both obvious and instructive, complete except in one respect: unlike Prometheus, who is eventually freed by Hercules, Frankenstein cannot be released from his torture. Although Walton and his ship offer a way of escape, Frankenstein knows that if he does not continue pursuing the monster, he will become the pursued. Unlike the mythical Prometheus, whose torture is merely physical, his modern counterpart must face the continual fear of psychological torment — a torment as chilling and destructive as the ice that is all around him. As a parable highlighting the dangers of pushing at the boundaries of scientific research, a journey of discovery that many scientists continue to take, the moral is starkly drawn.

Chapter summaries and notes

Volume One, Letters I–IV

Robert Walton is a 28-year-old sea captain who sets out from St Petersburg on a journey to the North Pole. He hopes to find a passage from the Pacific to the Atlantic. He writes a series of letters to his sister, Mrs Saville, in London. This expedition is his ultimate dream, and he is determined that it will succeed. He is worried that he has no friend on the trip to sustain him in his disappointment if it should not work out and to regulate his passions.

Once embarked on the voyage things are going well, when a strange sighting is made. In the middle of the ocean on sheets of floating ice a sleigh is seen. It is driven by what appears to be a human, but of enormous size. The figure disappears, leaving the whole crew in amazement. The next day another sleigh pulls up alongside the ship, on the brink of destruction now, amidst the ice. This time its driver is human and asks where the ship is bound. He boards the ship, nearly frozen and completely exhausted. It soon becomes evident that he is tracking the enormous figure Walton and his men have seen. Walton learns that the stranger, Victor Frankenstein, is deeply distressed, and when Walton explains the purpose of his trip to the north, the stranger becomes violently agitated and decides to tell Walton his own story to try to change Walton's mind.

Walton's letters provide the first part of his 'frame' narrative. Shelley uses these letters to introduce many of her key themes and techniques: journeys, pride, uncontrollable passions, madness, breaking accepted/acceptable boundaries, dreams, friendship, isolation, wild landscapes. She develops a clear sense of the parallels between Frankenstein and Walton.

Volume One, Chapter I

Frankenstein recounts his childhood in a wealthy and respected Swiss family. Born in Naples, Frankenstein was adored by his parents and he adored them; his childhood was idyllic. When he was 5 years old, his parents found and adopted an angelic orphan girl, living with a penniless Italian family. They raised her as their own. The child, named Elizabeth Lavenza, became Frankenstein's sister and the object almost of his worship. He considers her his most beautiful and most valued possession.

The focus is on the themes of family and kinship and the pain of isolation. As the product of a loving, almost ideal family, the reader expects that Frankenstein will reflect these qualities himself. Shelley introduces the idea of caring for children and the helpless; this later becomes important in relation to the monster.

Volume One, Chapter II

After the birth of their second son, Ernest, the Frankensteins move back to Switzerland. Victor Frankenstein has a small but intimate group of friends, including Henry Clerval and his beloved Elizabeth. Frankenstein introduces his passionate desire to learn the secrets of heaven and earth, foreshadowing his later downfall. For the moment, however, Elizabeth's presence restrains him somewhat. He becomes fascinated with the works of Paracelsus, Albertus Magnus and Cornelius Agrippa, a Roman alchemist. He shares their desire to penetrate the secrets of nature. He longs for glory, and is fascinated with how one might communicate with, or even raise, the dead. He becomes disillusioned with Agrippa and the others when he observes a lightning storm, a phenomenon which they are unable to explain.

We see Frankenstein's thirst for forbidden knowledge and his compulsive nature, which is close to madness. Elizabeth's 'saintly' nature contrasts with Frankenstein's 'dark' desires. The influence of femininity seems to offer potential salvation. Clerval's openness contrasts with Frankenstein's secretive nature, too. Frankenstein's curiosity goes unchecked and undirected by his father. Note the telling appearance of the lightning storm.

Volume One, Chapter III

At the age of 17, Frankenstein is sent to university at Ingolstadt. Shortly before he goes, his mother contracts scarlet fever and dies, expressing the wish that Frankenstein and Elizabeth should marry. Clerval wishes to accompany Frankenstein to Ingolstadt, but Clerval's father will not allow it. Frankenstein reflects upon the loneliness of his life at the university, but is excited at the possibility of learning. He is almost put off his studies by M. Krempe, who ridicules the study he has already undertaken, but is inspired by M. Waldman, who believes that scientists can perform miracles.

The marriage of Frankenstein and Elizabeth is foregrounded. Frankenstein finds himself isolated and 'unprotected' at Ingolstadt. Waldman's perception of the god-like status of scientists fuels Frankenstein's determination to pursue his studies.

Volume One, Chapter IV

Frankenstein becomes Waldman's protégé, and he secludes himself in the laboratories for extended periods of time. In 2 years, he pays not one visit to his family. He develops a consuming interest in the human frame and the life force. He pillages graveyards for body parts, practises vivisection and discovers the secret of how to generate life. He determines to fashion an enormous body and anticipates the day when a new race of beings will bless him as their creator. The days and nights and seasons pass without Frankenstein noticing. He grows pale and emaciated.

Frankenstein's obsession grows. He becomes increasingly isolated and yearns for god-like powers of omnipotence; he transgresses the boundaries of wise and acceptable research. He becomes increasingly monstrous and appears sub-human in the bloody pursuit of his studies. His declining physical condition reflects his declining moral stature.

Volume One, Chapter V

Frankenstein finally brings his creation to life. Far from being the beautiful creature he had imagined, it is hideous, and Frankenstein at once rushes to his room in horror and disgust. He has difficulty sleeping, and has terrible nightmares about Elizabeth and his mother. He wakes to find the creature staring at him fondly.

Frankenstein runs out of his apartment, leaving the creature alone, and unexpectedly meets Clerval, whose father has relented, as he arrives in Ingolstadt to start his studies. Frankenstein learns of the worries of his family, who have not heard from him for so long. He conceals his work from Clerval. The monster has left, but the next day Frankenstein falls violently ill. Clerval nurses him back to health. A letter awaits Frankenstein from Elizabeth.

The dreaming and waking worlds are blurred in this chapter — it is full of dreams and nightmares, some of which are fantasy and some of which are terribly real. Frankenstein's sickness of body symbolises his sickness of mind and morality. The creature's innocent and loving approaches to his creator contrast brutally with the rejection and horror Frankenstein feels towards the monster. Frankenstein's cruelty to the monster also contrasts with the kindness and care he receives from Clerval.

Volume One, Chapter VI

Elizabeth's letter updates Frankenstein on family matters and implores him to write as soon as possible. He resolves to write at once. Clerval, seeing Frankenstein's distaste for his laboratory, finds new accommodation and removes all his instruments. As the summer passes, Frankenstein decides to return to Geneva. This return is delayed, and he and Clerval undertake a walking tour during which Frankenstein seems to be returning to himself and his old love of nature.

Elizabeth's letter emphasises how complete Frankenstein's isolation in Ingolstadt has been. His sudden abandonment of science is clearly an attempt to deny the events of the last 2 years. He attempts to forget the existence of the creature to which he owes so much in the way of care and attention. He refuses to acknowledge his errors and false pride.

Volume One, Chapter VII

A letter from Frankenstein's father announces the murder of his youngest brother, William, and begs Frankenstein to return without delay. A locket has been stolen from his dead body, and this is the supposed motive. Full of fears, Frankenstein returns to Geneva, arriving in the midst of a terrific thunderstorm. A flash of lightning reveals an enormous figure lurking in some trees, and Frankenstein is at once certain that the monster is the murderer of his brother. He longs to pursue the creature and warn his family, but fears that they will reject his tale as mere madness. On finally reaching home, he learns that Justine Moritz, a trusted family servant, is to be tried for the murder.

A lightning storm (a staple device of Gothic horror) heralds the return of the monster. The storm symbolises the internal turmoil facing Frankenstein. His language towards the monster — 'deformity', 'wretch', 'filthy daemon' — sets the tone for their future relations.

Frankenstein disingenuously refuses to tell his tale of shame, on the grounds that it will be written off as madness, in order to protect himself and his reputation.

Volume One, Chapter VIII

Justine's trial commences. Frankenstein again considers speaking up in Justine's defence, but fails to do so. The evidence against her is compelling, especially her possession of the locket stolen from the body. This she is unable to explain. Elizabeth speaks passionately in Justine's defence, but it is not enough to prevent her being sentenced to death. In order to obtain absolution before she dies, Justine confesses to the crime in prison, even though she is innocent. Frankenstein selfishly considers his own plight to be worse than that of Justine.

Justine and William are the first innocent victims of Frankenstein's ambition. Even though unwilling to explain what he believes to be the truth, Frankenstein is not without feelings of guilt — he refers to 'fangs of remorse' tearing at him. He is isolated in his terrible suspicions of the truth. Like the monster, his ability to relate to human society is limited.

Volume Two, Chapter I

Frankenstein is tormented by guilt. The family retires to Belrive. He contemplates suicide and finds himself out of harmony with his magnificent surroundings. He nurtures a pathological hatred of his creation and thinks of nothing but revenge. Elizabeth now sees mankind as monsters; her views increase Frankenstein's pain. He takes a tour of the Chamounix valley to try to escape his emotional turmoil.

Frankenstein is isolated emotionally, caught between his hatred of the monster and his love of his family, both of which are equally painful to him. Nature plays a key role: the awesome, God-revealing natural world that Frankenstein loves is ironically set against his unnatural rejection of that order in setting himself up as God through his scientific researches. Elizabeth's view of men as monsters tellingly questions whether it is Frankenstein or his creature that is truly monstrous.

Volume Two, Chapter II

Frankenstein continues his tour of Chamounix. He climbs Montanvert, where he calls on the 'wandering spirits' to help him. At this the monster appears. Frankenstein, in fury, threatens to kill him, but the monster remains rational and asks Frankenstein to help him in his misery, threatening bloody revenge if he fails to do so. The monster is eloquent in presenting his intrinsically good nature and his pitiful isolation in the world. He begs Frankenstein to hear his story.

Frankenstein seeks escape in the rugged wilderness of the mountains. The meeting between creator and creature is loaded with biblical and Miltonic references to the story of Adam, Satan and God.

Volume Two, Chapter III

The monster recounts his early development and awareness of the world around him. Tormented by want, the monster resides in the forests near Ingolstadt. As he travels in search of food and shelter, whenever he comes in contact with humans he suffers maltreatment, in spite of his efforts to befriend them. He finally takes refuge in a hovel by a cottage, where he spends his time observing the inhabitants, the de Laceys.

In this chapter, we enter the heart of the novel — the monster's narrative. Shelley emphasises the early innocence and good nature of the monster, which contrasts with the humans he meets and their treatment of him. The monster's innocence and capacity for love is gradually being undermined. Isolation is emphasised.

Volume Two, Chapter IV

The monster grows to admire and love the de Lacey family, helping them however he can, in secret. He tries to learn their language. He realises that they are unhappy, but cannot understand why — they possess everything he lacks: love, shelter, companionship. One day, seeing his reflection in a pool, the monster becomes aware of his hideousness, but continues to hope to win them over by the beauty of his soul.

The creature longs to join human society. In comparing himself to the de Laceys, the creature feels himself to be a monster. Shelley builds the pathos as the monster continues to dream of acceptance by humans.

Volume Two, Chapter V

A beautiful stranger arrives at the cottage. It is Safie, Felix de Lacey's sweetheart. In teaching her their language, the family unwittingly teaches the monster too. From the history book they use, the creature learns of the true, cruel nature of humanity and despairs of gaining the acceptance of the cottagers.

The monster's attractive humanity becomes clear. In Safie we are presented with yet another outsider. The monstrosity of human society is emphasised, leading to the monster's despair — both he and Frankenstein are estranged by what they know.

Volume Two, Chapter VI

The monster at last learns the family's name and history. Trying to help Safie and her father, imprisoned on account of their race in Paris, the family lost their place in society. Safie was promised in marriage to Felix, but upon gaining freedom her father betrayed Felix and Felix's father and sister were imprisoned. They were forced to live in exile in Germany. Safie escaped her father and found her lover.

Shelley places further emphasis on betrayal and the position of the outsider. The story reflects both the goodness and evil of which humans are capable.

Volume Two, Chapter VII

The monster discovers Milton's *Paradise Lost*, Plutarch's *Lives* and Goethe's *The Sorrows of Young Werther*. He believes them to be works of fact, and particularly relates Milton's story to his own position and his relationship with Frankenstein. Winter comes, and the monster decides to speak to the cottagers. When the young people are out, he goes in and speaks to the blind old man. All goes well until the return of Felix and the others, who drive him away.

The books give the monster a way of 'reading' his own situation. He now knows the extent to which he is rejected, a fact driven home by his rejection by the de Laceys. Good and evil are brought to the fore in both the monster's and the reader's minds. His goodness and love have been met with evil and irrational hatred.

Volume Two, Chapter VIII

The monster curses his creator for giving him life and declares war on mankind as his revenge. A final effort to engage with the de Laceys is foiled, as they have fled, and he burns their cottage to the ground. He decides to travel to Geneva to exact his revenge. Further encounters, even with innocent children, serve only to confirm what he has already learnt. On arriving near Geneva, he meets another child, who turns out to be William, Frankenstein's brother. The monster kills him and steals his locket, which he later hides on Justine Moritz as she sleeps in a barn. At the end of his tale, the monster demands that Frankenstein create a companion for him, so he will no longer be alone.

The burning of the cottage is an externalisation of the fire of revenge now burning in the monster's heart. The violence of the landscapes he passes through and of the elements further reflect the monster's state of mind.

Volume Two, Chapter IX

Frankenstein returns as narrator. Initially he refuses to consider the monster's demand, fearing that the monster and his companion may destroy the world. The monster argues that he is destructive only because of his enforced isolation and loneliness. Frankenstein is full of doubts, but sees the justness of the creature's demands and feels some compassion for him. He decides to comply with the monster's wishes and the monster promises to watch his progress with eagerness. Frankenstein returns to Geneva.

The monster remains reasonable and controlled in a way that Frankenstein cannot match. The monster is aware that he is more powerful than his creator and is therefore, in a sense, the master. In conceding to the creature's demands, Frankenstein accepts implicit guilt for his previous actions.

Volume Three, Chapter I

Weeks pass, and Frankenstein cannot steel himself to begin his dreadful task. He determines to go to England to undertake the necessary study and work. Pressurised by his father to fulfil his dying mother's wishes, Frankenstein agrees to marry Elizabeth on his return. He sets off on his journey with Clerval as a companion, continually aware of the haunting presence of the monster, who has vowed to watch his progress. Frankenstein is painfully aware of the differences between himself and Clerval.

The marriage with Elizabeth is foregrounded once more. Frankenstein's forthcoming union parallels the monster's anticipated union with a new companion; the two are linked inextricably in the reader's mind. Frankenstein is as bound to the monster and his promise as a slave.

Volume Three, Chapter II

After a protracted tour through England, Frankenstein and Clerval visit Scotland. Frankenstein leaves Clerval visiting friends and takes a cottage on a remote, barren island to complete his second creation.

Frankenstein's ability to take pleasure is blasted. He is increasingly aware of his separation from the rest of mankind.

Volume Three, Chapter III

Frankenstein contemplates the possible outcomes of his compliance with the monster's wishes. Looking to the window, he sees the grinning face of the monster watching him, and then and there destroys the body he is creating. The creature disappears, but returns several hours later to reproach Frankenstein. He expresses the central paradox of their relationship: 'You are my creator, but I am your master.' The monster leaves, vowing to be with Frankenstein on his wedding night. Frankenstein disposes of the body at sea, but drifts on the current, landing on the Irish coast, where he is arrested on suspicion of the murder of a man whose body has been washed up on shore.

Frankenstein's terrible dilemma encapsulates the division between the humanitarian and the selfish in his nature. He falsely and inexplicably refers all the monster's warnings to himself. The confusion between creator and creature, master and slave is multiplied.

Volume Three, Chapter IV

Frankenstein is taken before the magistrate and shown the body of Clerval, his supposed victim. For 2 months, Frankenstein is stricken with delirium. During his illness, the magistrate has sent for Frankenstein's father, who travels to Ireland. Frankenstein insists on returning to Geneva at once to protect the rest of his family.

Note the close parallels between Frankenstein's 'murder' of the monster's companion and the murder of Clerval. Note too how Shelley prepares the way for the murder of Elizabeth.

Volume Three, Chapter V

On their journey home, Frankenstein tells his father that he is the engineer of all the tragedy that has befallen the family, but the father attributes this confession to his son's delirium. Frankenstein recalls the monster's promise to be with him on his wedding night, but decides not to delay his marriage to Elizabeth. He deceives himself that he can avert the monster's threats and live happily with Elizabeth.

Frankenstein's self-delusion and solipsism are key here. He persists in believing that the monster's threat is to him. Note Shelley's juxtaposition of happiness and a brooding sense of foreboding. Note too the comparison to Adam and Eve that Frankenstein draws, alerting readers to the inevitable presence of Satan/the monster.

Volume Three, Chapter VI

Frankenstein and Elizabeth arrive in Como. Frankenstein, certain that either he or the creature will die that night, sends Elizabeth to bed to try to protect her. Too late he hears her death screams. When he recovers from his shock, he embraces the dead Elizabeth, then sees the monster at the window, gloating over his grief. A search for the monster fails. Frankenstein's father dies shortly after hearing the news. Frankenstein admits all to a half-believing magistrate, but is left to pursue his revenge alone.

Note the use of the natural world to reflect events. Frankenstein is blinded by his solipsism to the true intentions of the monster. Frankenstein and his monster are drawn closer together than ever — both are isolated, consumed with revenge and the desire to destroy.

Volume Three, Chapter VII

Frankenstein vows eternal revenge and prepares to leave Geneva. He visits the graves of his family and calls upon the 'wandering ministers of vengeance' and the spirits of the dead to aid him. He is watched and taunted by the monster. For months he pursues his creation, until at last he sights it on the northern ocean. On the point of catching the monster, the ice breaks and he is adrift on an ice floe, when he is rescued by Walton. He begs Walton to kill the monster if he appears.

Revenge invigorates and intoxicates Frankenstein. He buries guilt in anger.

Walton, *in continuation*

Walton questions Frankenstein on how he created life. Frankenstein grows agitated and begs Walton to learn from his (Frankenstein's) mistakes. Walton becomes increasingly attached to Frankenstein. Meanwhile, the ship is every day in greater danger from encroaching ice. Walton is unwilling to accept the crew's desire to return if the ice breaks. Frankenstein is torn between the desire to save Walton from his fate and the urge to enlist his assistance in pursuing revenge, and offers a range of contradictory pleas and advice. Frankenstein dies, stating his conduct has been blameless. That night, the monster steals onto the ship and laments over the corpse of Frankenstein, aware, in Frankenstein's death, of the pain his acts of revenge have caused. Walton meets the monster and is unable to express the ambiguity of his emotions. The monster jumps from the ship, intending to burn himself alive at the North Pole.

Frankenstein appears to have learnt nothing from his sufferings and dies desiring revenge and still extolling the possibilities of scientific research. It is uncertain whether Walton will learn his lesson or not. The monster alone shows firm evidence of moral betterment. The novel ends with the suggestive combination of fire and ice.

Characters and pairings

Shelley's use of character

In beginning to consider the characters of the novel, it is as well to remember that *Frankenstein* is a text that works with (if not exactly within) the parameters of the Gothic genre. Any genre develops its own typical features and particular requirements. In the following passage David Punter writes of the stereotypical characters of Gothic novels:

> The world in which it did deal was peopled with stock characters, who discoursed in predictable ways: the shy, nervous, retiring heroine, who was nevertheless usually possessed of a remarkable ability to survive hideously dangerous situations; the heavy-handed, tyrannical father; the cast of comic extras and servants who, like many of the other characters, often seem to be lifted wholesale out of Jacobean drama; and above all the villain. The villain was always the most complex and interesting character in Gothic fiction, even when drawn with a clumsy hand: awe-inspiring, endlessly resourceful in pursuit of his often opaquely evil ends, and yet possessed of a mysterious attractiveness, he stalks from the pages of one Gothic novel to another, manipulating the doom of others while the knowledge of his own eventual fate surrounds him like the monastic habit and cowl which he so often wore.
>
> (David Punter, 1996)

A comparison of the main figures of the novel against these ideas is essential in beginning to understand how Shelley's presentation of character works with and differs from the generic norm.

Victor Frankenstein

Victor Frankenstein is a complex and fascinating character. In the first instance, the reader has some difficulty in deciding whether he fulfils the role of hero or whether he is an anti-hero. While his ends are evil, we may question whether they are 'opaquely' so, as in many ways Frankenstein is more misguided and deluded than actually evil. He is far from being the conventional villain of the Gothic world, displaying all too clearly the weaknesses and frailties of his nature. He is, however, indirectly responsible for causing the doom of his entire family and the monster he has created. Throughout the novel we gain a strange sense of the relationship between Frankenstein and the typical Gothic hero-villain, a role which he curiously subverts.

There is a distinct sense in which Frankenstein also relates to the figure of the Gothic heroine. Gothic novels often focus on the perspective of the heroine, exploring the psychological impact of repeated terror, horror and stress upon her (or, more rarely, him). Typically the impact of events is manifested in bodily and mental breakdown. As Frankenstein suffers his just deserts at the hands of the monster, his mental and physical decay are evident to the reader. Immediately after the successful creation of the monster, for example, he breaks down entirely, only surviving thanks to the good graces of his friend Clerval. As a study in the psychological impact of the terrible and the horrible, this confusion of the roles of hero/villain/heroine in Frankenstein is both profound and compelling.

The monster

Like Frankenstein, the monster is a complex and fascinating character. There are strong arguments for seeing his character as an extension of that of his creator, an idea explored at greater length in the 'Man and monster' section of this book (pp. 49–56). As with Frankenstein, the monster's role is strikingly ambiguous: to what extent are we to perceive him as the traditional villain and to what extent are we to see him as the victim of the piece? There is no doubt that as the novel progresses he grows increasingly villainous and malign, manipulating the doom of others with a certain gloating satisfaction in his insatiable pursuit of revenge on his creator. The motivation for his actions, however, must tend to mitigate our view of what he does. In many ways he is the helpless and friendless victim, a role traditionally given within the framework of Gothic to a young woman or child.

Elizabeth Lavenza

Elizabeth Lavenza is clearly the heroine. Her role, however, like so many of the characters in the novel, bears certain striking discrepancies from the conventions of Gothic. Unlike her counterparts in the works of Ann Radcliffe and Matthew Lewis, for example, Elizabeth's role is comparatively small (at times almost marginal, in the sense that she is rarely centre-stage); like them she must eventually and inevitably suffer (indeed, she suffers silently her neglect by Frankenstein and the pains that result from his thoughtless actions throughout the novel), but the main focus of the text is not her ordeals, but rather those faced by Frankenstein, her supposed protector and hero, within whose suffering her own is subsumed. She is an undeniably strong woman, far stronger — the reader suspects — than Frankenstein himself, who faces the repeated trials imposed upon her by Frankenstein with an unswerving loyalty and heroic resolve.

The horrific image of her white-clad body draped across the marital bed after her murder on the wedding night is one of pure Gothic sensation, however, and a turning point in the reader's understanding of Elizabeth's role. It is at this point that the reader is forced to reconsider the role Elizabeth has played and to realise that she has in fact been the typical Gothic heroine of her own novel, a novel which has been running parallel to the tale Frankenstein has told us, in which she is the victim of male neglect and systematic cruelty from the one man she should have been able to rely upon.

Henry Clerval

Clerval is significant in embodying many of the heroic qualities lacking in Frankenstein. Like the monster and Walton, he needs to be seen alongside the central figure of Frankenstein. He draws on some of the characteristics of the good male of Gothic fiction, the man (usually young and good-looking) who attempts to save the heroine from the trials to which she is subjected.

Captain Walton

Walton can be seen as something of the dashing, Romantic hero. He is clearly a representation of what Frankenstein used to be before his terrible confrontation with the monster. He fulfils a typical role within the realms of Gothic fiction, appearing as a younger, 'innocent' version of the hero.

Pairings

In the course of the novel, Shelley, like Emily Brontë in *Wuthering Heights*, Robert Louis Stevenson in *Dr Jekyll and Mr Hyde* and many other authors of Gothic, makes extensive use of pairs of characters. These pairings are not necessarily fixed; indeed, they shift frequently as the novel progresses, creating a range of different effects, pointing out both similarities and differences between the characters so paired. The following pairings are all highly significant in the course of the novel. The most important of all, that of Frankenstein and the monster, is dealt with separately in the 'Man and monster' section of this guide (pp. 49–56).

Frankenstein and Walton

Both men are dreamers, blinded to the complete truth and impact of what they are seeking to do by the all-encompassing nature of their fantasies. Shelley is concerned from the outset that the reader's view of Frankenstein (who may otherwise appear as an insane and extreme scientific renegade) should be filtered through the apparently more rational figure of Walton. While he shares

Frankenstein's obsessive personality and desire to reach new heights (or depths) of scientific research, Walton is as yet comparatively 'innocent' and unaware of the potential consequences of his actions. This pairing prepares the reader to accept the transformation that occurs in Frankenstein from the scientist with a dream to the fear-crazed madman Walton encounters on the ice. An almost spiritual closeness exists between Walton and Frankenstein. Walton senses immediately in Frankenstein a kindred spirit; however, we must note that the friendship Walton describes cannot be forged with Frankenstein in his current state — it is the former Frankenstein who might have proved a fit companion for him. This serves to illustrate the imminent and disturbing danger facing Walton should he continue along the path he is currently treading. Both Walton and Frankenstein have difficulties with self-control, single-mindedly pursuing their dreams even in the face of warnings to the contrary. As such, Frankenstein's tale is a moral and cautionary lesson for Walton.

The closeness between the two men is driven home at the end of the novel, when Frankenstein seeks to use Walton as an extension of himself in his mad pursuit of the monster. Although Walton, at the near-mutinous insistence of his crew, does not pursue the monster as Frankenstein wished, the question of his future as a man and a scientist remains distinctly uncertain. Frankenstein, in spite of all that has happened to him, holds open the possibility that science and other scientists may achieve where he has failed. Thus, while he seems to be warning Walton away from the dangers he himself has experienced and the punishment he has suffered, he ambiguously holds out the 'carrot' of further exploration. If Walton is like Frankenstein in so many respects, as Shelley has led the reader to believe he is, then there is a distinct possibility that he will prove to be like Frankenstein in his insatiable hope of succeeding in the face of all the odds.

Frankenstein and Elizabeth

While there are essential and striking contrasts between the natures of Elizabeth and Frankenstein, their pairing is very important. First as brother and adoptive 'sister', then as an affianced couple, and finally within the (albeit very brief) union of marriage, the reader is obviously required to consider in detail the implications of this pairing. As has been suggested before, Frankenstein is a curiously 'incomplete' character; his is a deeply flawed personality and, like Walton, he is forever in need of the guidance of wise companions. Elizabeth is one of the most significant of these, and should be one of the most intimate. With her strength of character, her indefatigable loyalty and her seemingly endless patience, she makes the perfect foil to Frankenstein's weakness and indiscipline, his waywardness and frequent indiscretions. It is Frankenstein's tragedy, and Elizabeth's, that Frankenstein never appreciates fully the worth of the 'gift' he has in Elizabeth. In persistently overlooking and undervaluing her (for vast quantities of the novel the couple are hundreds, even thousands of miles apart) and the goodness and wisdom she stands for, he effectively seals their fates as individuals and as a couple. In his supremely egotistical inability (or unwillingness) to understand the nature of the monster's threats and the depth of his need for a worthy companion (something Frankenstein himself fails to value, as his treatment of Elizabeth makes clear), he ensures the death of the person he claims to value most.

Frankenstein is a novel that emphasises the importance of balance and completeness. Elizabeth offers the perfect (and tragically spurned) completion and balance to Victor's personality.

Frankenstein and Clerval

As friends from childhood, Frankenstein and Clerval offer the reader another important pairing. Both are ardent for knowledge; like Frankenstein, Clerval wishes to attend the university to pursue his studies. Unlike Frankenstein, however, whose early dabblings in science go effectively uncorrected by his indulgent father, Clerval is not allowed to attend at first. Both men have inquisitive and lively minds and both imagine a glorious and renowned future for themselves, but Clerval, perhaps on account of the intervention of his father, which at first seems unduly harsh, is better able to regulate his desires. This becomes clear when, on finally overcoming his father's objections and arriving at Ingolstadt to pursue his studies, he puts off his long-awaited dreams to nurse Frankenstein through his sickness in the wake of the creation of the monster. Clerval's nature includes the caring, loving and devoted dimensions that Frankenstein's lacks, or which are eclipsed by an almost solipsistic introversion.

Secondary pairings

Frankenstein and Justine Moritz

Both are falsely accused of committing a murder perpetrated by the monster. Through this similarity in their stories (a parallel to which Frankenstein is crushingly alert) she becomes a measure of Frankenstein's conscience, a symbol of the destruction of innocence he has caused. Her death and his inability to prove her innocence (and unwillingness even to try, as Elizabeth does) points to the very heart of Frankenstein's nature and the terrible dilemma he faces.

Elizabeth and Walton

Walton, like Elizabeth, has an early love of poety, notably Homer and Shakespeare (a characteristic both share with Clerval). This may serve to suggest some kind of redeeming feature in Walton's character. Both are closely bound to Frankenstein — Elizabeth as his 'other half' and Walton as a 'kindred spirit'.

Walton and the monster

The monster, a present reality for Frankenstein, is very much an imminent possibility for Walton. If we accept that the monster can be seen as a symbol of where irresponsible scientific exploration and 'madness' may lead, then he is as much a part of Walton's make-up as he is of Frankenstein's. In this respect it is worth observing that Walton sights the monster before he meets Frankenstein, significantly suggesting the presence of the monster in him before Frankenstein arrives to offer an explanation.

Clerval and Elizabeth

Both Elizabeth and Clerval are poetry lovers, a characteristic which seems to indicate a civilising influence within the novel. Both suffer extremely because of their love for Frankenstein, showing the greatest personal dedication and even sacrifice for his sake. Both also seek to regulate Frankenstein's nature, with an equal lack of success.

Elizabeth and the monster's destroyed companion

Clear and significant parallels exist here. Elizabeth, as Frankenstein's bride, is obviously comparable with the potential 'bride' of the monster. Likewise, when Frankenstein destroys the monster's companion, to balance the narrative and to complete the parallels between the monster and his creator, Elizabeth must suffer the same fate as the monster's 'bride'. Although they contrast on the surface (Elizabeth a picture of beauty and the monster's companion likely to be as ugly as the monster), they come together to symbolise the importance of companionship, whether given or taken away.

Doubling of plot devices

It is not only in her use of characters that Shelley employs the device of doubling. Throughout the novel there are examples of the doubling of plot devices. Listed below are some key examples of this:

- false accusations of murder against both Justine and Frankenstein
- the dumping of the monster's companion and Clerval in the Irish Sea
- Frankenstein's scientific exploration and Walton's scientific voyage
- the monster's rejection by society and the de Laceys' rejection
- the destruction of the monster's companion and of Elizabeth
- the traitorous betrayal of the monster by Frankenstein and the betrayal of the de Laceys by Safie's father

Furthermore, the whole novel doubles the plots (or elements of the plots) of 'The Rime of the Ancient Mariner', *Paradise Lost* and the Prometheus myth.

The extent of Shelley's doubling links to one of the greatest fears portrayed in Gothic fiction, that of a cyclical repetition of the events of terror and horror

portrayed. Through her use of repetition and mutation, Shelley suggests the inevitable and inescapable nature of what she portrays.

Character sketches

When approaching any work of fiction it is essential to draw together your thoughts about a particular character and his or her role within the text. The following list suggests key questions to consider:

- Why have they been included?
- How do they connect to the themes and concerns of the novel as a whole?
- How do they relate to those around them?
- How do they use language? How do they act?
- How do others act towards them and speak about them?

With the exceptions of Frankenstein and the monster (dealt with in the 'Man and monster' section of this guide (pp. 49–56)), the following pages suggest areas for consideration of the central characters in Frankenstein.

Major characters

Walton — ambitious; unchecked; isolated from friends and family; enchanted by prospects of exploration; blinded to danger of his path; rapidly forms devotion to Frankenstein; idealistic; naïve; headstrong; selfish; passionate; determined; enthusiastic — all characteristics that link him to Frankenstein. Shelley prepares the reader, through Walton, for the characteristics they will encounter, at a far more advanced stage, in Frankenstein, who is unable to control his emotions and feelings fully.

Elizabeth — angelic; beautiful; an orphan; patient; kind; self-effacing; loving; idealised; a form of perfection; a creature set apart; idolised by Frankenstein; 'the beautiful and adored companion of all my occupations and my pleasures'; Frankenstein is strongly possessive of Elizabeth; build-up of 'holy' language is attached to Elizabeth; she becomes increasingly downcast as Frankenstein distances himself from her.

Clerval — ambitious; more 'obedient' to father than Frankenstein; noble; inspired by learning; devoted; honest; generous. 'Soaring ambition' is also a characteristic — like Frankenstein; like Frankenstein and Walton, he needs the moderating hand of friendship, provided by Elizabeth.

Secondary characters

Frankenstein Senior — loving and caring; emotional; fails to control Frankenstein's budding scientific ambition; his parenting contrasts with Frankenstein's 'parenting' of the monster.

Frankenstein's mother — loving; caring; a powerful influence, even after death, on her family and Frankenstein in particular.

Justine Moritz — upright; devoted; her unjust accusation of murder parallels Frankenstein's unjust accusation of having murdered Clerval.

The de Laceys — outsiders; kind and caring; ultimate rejection of monster.

Safie — outsider; exotic stranger; determined; devoted.

William — innocent victim; shows how even children reject the monster.

M. Krempe — disliked by Frankenstein; almost unwittingly 'saves' Frankenstein.

M. Waldman — passionate scientist; wins Frankenstein for science.

Man and monster

The monstrous

This is an important concept within the novel. The reader needs to consider in detail a variety of ways in which we can look at Frankenstein, his monster, and the relationship that exists between them. To begin with, look at the following ways in which Shelley plays with the idea of the monstrous in the novel:

- She suggests that there are 'monsters' in men (and the knowledge of men) which can be released into the world.
- She shows us the monstrous nature of man's behaviour.
- She uses monstrous crimes.
- She looks at the boundaries between man and monster, which are not always as distinct as the reader would like to think.
- She questions the nature of Frankenstein's creation, which, though physically monstrous, becomes morally and behaviourally wicked only as a direct result of the treatment it receives from humans.
- She is eager to point out the 'monstrous' treatment the monster receives from humans.
- She questions the nature of perception of the monstrous — while 'creating' his monster, Frankenstein is convinced of its beauty.
- The humans, with the temporary exception of M. de Lacey (who in his blindness is the only human capable of truly seeing the value and personality of the monster), reject the monster as without question barbarous and sub-human on the basis of its physical appearance alone.

These ideas offer the reader a wealth of potential approaches to interpreting the events of the novel and the behaviour of the characters within it, as well as the views of the author herself.

Frankenstein: man or monster? Quotations and analysis

When approaching any quotation it is essential to evaluate its validity and significance in relation both to the text as a whole and to the argument being formed. For each quotation below, consider the following points:

- identify who the speakers are and the context in which they are speaking

- consider what they suggest about both Frankenstein and, where appropriate, the speaker
- evaluate their relationship to the themes of the novel
- think about how they link to events in the novel
- find other examples to support the views expressed

(1)   His limbs were nearly frozen, and his body dreadfully emaciated by fatigue and suffering. I never saw a man in so wretched a condition. (p. 26)

Frankenstein's physical condition contrasts strikingly to the huge form of the monster Walton has previously seen. His body symbolises the impact that his hate-fuelled pursuit of the monster has had upon him as a human. His desperate position illustrates his extremity and isolation.

(2)   I never saw a more interesting creature; his eyes have generally an expression of wildness, and even madness, but there are moments when…his whole countenance is lighted up, as it were, with a beam of benevolence and sweetness that I never saw equalled. (p. 27)

This observation illustrates the complex and contrasting nature of the character of Frankenstein. Walton introduces the questionable sanity of Frankenstein, an idea of central significance in terms of his relations with the monster. Even in extremity, however, we note that he retains some of his more attractive human characteristics. This offers a clear example of Frankenstein as an image of fallen man.

(3)   Such a man has a double existence: he may suffer misery and be overwhelmed by disappoint-ments, yet, when he has retired into himself, he will be like a celestial spirit, that has a halo around him, within whose circle no grief or folly ventures. (p. 30)

This passage overtly identifies the double nature of Frankenstein. It is almost as if he has a split personality. The warring elements of the human and the divine, the bodily and the spiritual link here to the frequent use of the doppelgänger in Gothic fiction. Such notions are also linked closely to a Freudian reading of the novel.

(4)   Every night I was oppressed by a slow fever, and I became nervous to a most painful degree; the fall of a leaf startled me, and I shunned my fellow-creatures as if I had been guilty of a crime. Sometimes I grew alarmed at the wreck I perceived that I had become; the energy of my purpose alone sustained me… (p. 57)

Here the reader sees a profound, even obsessive self-awareness in Frankenstein. It also marks out a determination to press on in the face of adversity. A growing sense of fear, tension and foreboding becomes clear.

(5)   Anguish and despair had penetrated into the core of my heart; I bore a hell within me which nothing could extinguish. (p. 89)

Anguish and despair are key markers in any character; the loss of hope this signifies is integral in the events that follow, as Frankenstein becomes increasingly unable to control himself, moving under a series of external compulsions. This passage also indicates the beginnings of guilt and realisation of what he has done, although such emotions are never developed fully and recognised within him.

(6) Sometimes, with my sails set, I was carried by the wind; and sometimes, after rowing into the middle of the lake, I left the boat to pursue its own course, and gave way to my own miserable reflections. (p. 94)

This excerpt illustrates Frankenstein's separation from his family. It also emphasises the extent to which he allows himself to drift at the mercy of forces greater than himself. This identifies for the reader a sense of powerlessness and purposelessness in Frankenstein, perhaps as a result of his growing despair and fatalism.

(7) ...often, I say, I was tempted to plunge into the silent lake, that the waters might close over me and my calamities forever. (p. 94)

This shows the depths to which Frankenstein has sunk. From the proud and arrogant young scientist, he now verges on the suicidal (note once again the wealth of Freudian overtones in his desire for self-annihilation and the suggestively womb-like waters of the lake). This desire for death, even at his own hands, later links him to the monster, who wishes to end his life and outlines his intentions to do so at the end of the novel.

(8) My haggard and wild appearance awoke intense alarm. ... I felt as if I were placed under a ban — as if I had no right to claim their sympathies — as if never more might I enjoy companionship with them. (p. 151)

Frankenstein identifies his sense of separation from his family. He extends this to encompass his loss of the right to be considered part of humanity. This connects him significantly to the monster, who is universally rejected by humanity. He later goes on to elaborate on this idea, seeing himself as 'a miserable wretch, haunted by a curse that shut up every avenue to enjoyment'. His perception of separation becomes increasingly absolute as the novel progresses until he sees 'an insurmountable barrier placed between me and my fellow-men', suggesting a steady move away from humanity and towards the monstrous.

(9) I am a blasted tree; the bolt has entered my soul... (p. 165)

This quotation links significantly to an earlier image of the blasted tree, when the young Frankenstein saw the destruction of a tree by lightning. Through the deployment of this image, Shelley links Frankenstein's destruction as a human to the initial germ of an idea that led to his scientific explorations.

(10) I felt as if I had committed some great crime, the consciousness of which haunted me. I was guiltless, but I had indeed drawn down a horrible curse upon my head, as mortal as that of crime. (p. 167)

Here Frankenstein seems to try to absolve himself of guilt. As readers we find this question far more ambiguous. We cannot simply share Frankenstein's conviction that he is not guilty of a crime, against himself, against God, against the order of the natural world, against the monster and against humanity.

Pairing: Frankenstein and the monster

Throughout the novel Shelley makes use of the device of pairing. This is a technique frequently used in texts from the Gothic genre, another famous example being Robert Louis Stevenson's *Dr Jekyll and Mr Hyde*. Typically an ostensibly 'good' character is shadowed by a more sinister, even ghostly, double, or doppelgänger, which is usually taken to represent the darker potential of their nature. The most striking and extended use of this device is Frankenstein and the monster. Both Frankenstein and the monster begin life with the potential for good, but find their lives turned to evil. The significance of this pairing is elaborated and emphasised as Shelley develops a complex series of parallels between the creator and his creature. As Frankenstein dumps the body of his aborted companion for the monster in the sea, so the monster dumps the body of Clerval in the sea. Both Frankenstein and the monster find themselves increasingly isolated from the companionship of mankind. Both rebel against their creators. Both share the physical hardship and torment of their ceaseless pursuit across Europe, a vengeful pursuit which consumes both the body and the spirit, so that Frankenstein's emaciated form makes him almost as sub-human and monstrous as his creation. The mutually destructive passion that fires both man and monster reaches its heights of vindictive fury in the destruction of their respective 'brides'. Both are guilty of committing crimes against humanity, which they have to pay for in their increasing isolation and consuming guilt. Through these extended parallels, the two characters are tied to each other inseparably. Indeed, such is the coincidence of detail woven by Shelley that the reader finds the distinctions between Frankenstein and the monster increasingly blurred — to the extent that they become all but indistinguishable at times.

Quotations on monstrosity

Frankenstein, the monster, and humankind in general are all portrayed as at times capable of 'monstrosity'.

(1)   …a being which had the shape of a man, but apparently of gigantic stature, sat in the sledge and guided the dogs. (p. 25)

Walton's first sighting of the monster emphasises both the similarities and the differences between the monster and humans.

(2)   My mother's tender caresses and my father's smile of benevolent pleasure while regarding me are my first recollections. I was their plaything and their idol, and something better — their child, the innocent and helpless creature bestowed on them by Heaven, whom to bring up

to good, and whose future lot it was in their hands to direct to happiness or misery, according as they fulfilled their duties towards me. (p. 35)

Frankenstein recalls his childhood and the extent to which he was nurtured and cared for by his parents. This passage should be compared and contrasted to the shameful lack of nurturing he is prepared to give his own 'child' after he has given it life. It raises questions of duty.

(3) I beheld the wretch — the miserable monster whom I had created. He held up the curtain of the bed; and his eyes, if eyes they may be called, were fixed on me. His jaws opened, and he uttered some inarticulate sounds, while a grin wrinkled his cheeks. He might have spoken, but I did not hear; one hand was stretched out, seemingly to detain me, but I escaped and rushed downstairs. (p. 59)

The monster is portrayed as a baby. Shelley presents it in an appealing light, foregrounding its innocent and defenceless nature, which contrasts with its callous rejection by Frankenstein. The reader is forced to weigh up who appears to be the genuine monster in this episode.

(4) I could not be mistaken. A flash of lightning illuminated the object, and discovered its shape plainly to me; its gigantic stature, and the deformity of its aspect, more hideous than belongs to humanity, instantly informed me that it was the wretch, the filthy daemon to whom I had given life. (pp. 77–78)

Note Frankenstein's perception of his creation as sub-human. Observe too his use of vocabulary of hell and evil in relation to the monster.

(5) Alas, I had turned loose into the world a depraved wretch, whose delight was in carnage and misery... (p. 78)

Frankenstein fails to see that it is his own monstrous neglect of his creation that has turned it into a monster. He has no sense at this stage of his responsibility for what has happened.

(6) I considered the being whom I had cast among mankind, and endowed with the will and power to effect purposes of horror, such as the deed he had now done, nearly in the light of my own vampire, my own spirit let loose from the grave, and forced to destroy all that was dear to me. (p. 78)

Frankenstein speaks of the monster in terms that suggest their interdependence, as creator and creature. This strengthens the concept of the doppelgänger which is so key to the novel. Frankenstein's recognition makes all the more astounding his selfish inability to see the monster's subsequent intentions in his revenge, when he seeks to destroy Frankenstein not by violence against him personally, but through violence against his immediate family and loved ones.

(7) I wandered like an evil spirit, for I had committed deeds of mischief beyond description horrible, and more, much more (I persuaded myself) was yet behind. Yet my heart overflowed with kindness, and the love of virtue... (p. 93)

Frankenstein compares himself to the archetypal Gothic figure of the wanderer (Melmoth the Wanderer, the Wandering Jew, Count Dracula, and the monster are all condemned to wander without finding rest). This extract identifies too the contrasting powers and influences in the life of Frankenstein. Note his similarity to the monster — both began life with the capacity and intention for good.

(8) '...now misery has come home, and men appear to me as monsters thirsting for each other's blood'. (p. 95)

Elizabeth here reflects, in the light of William's murder and Justine Moritz's wrongful execution, on the monstrous potential of humanity.

(9) ...the fiend that lurked in my heart. (p. 96)

By extension, it is Frankenstein's ambition and neglect embodied in the monster that causes the danger to humanity. The reader must question to what he is in fact referring here — is it the monster? His scientific research? The knowledge of his guilt for the deaths of William and Justine? An unacknowledged, prescient awareness of what the monster may yet go on to do? An awareness that he has contravened the will/the role of God as creator?

(10) I suddenly beheld the figure of a man, at some distance, advancing towards me with superhuman speed. He bounded over the crevices in the ice, among which I had walked with caution... (p. 101)

Note the shift in emphasis in the rest of this passage, from 'man' to 'superhuman' to 'the wretch'. This passage illuminates Frankenstein's view of the monster, which is full of contradictions and complexity.

(11) ...his countenance bespoke bitter anguish, combined with disdain and malignity, while its unearthly ugliness rendered it almost too horrible for human eyes. (p. 102)

Shelley here identifies a complex mixture of characteristics in the monster, arousing an equally complex response in the reader.

(12) 'Do your duty towards me, and I will do mine towards you and the rest of mankind.' (p. 102)

This illustrates clearly the interdependence of the creature and its creator. It is a lack of sense of duty that leads to monstrosity in the novel.

(13) 'I will not be tempted to set myself in opposition to thee. I am thy creature, and I will be even mild and docile to my natural lord and king, if thou wilt also perform thy part, the which thou owest me.' (pp. 102–03)

Here the monster demonstrates considerably more respect and restraint than does Frankenstein. His speech is more reasoned and reasonable and his ideas formed more fully. The reader is obliged to consider who appears monstrous here: the monster who asks for care and affection, or the creator who refuses to be kind, responsible and dutiful to his creature.

(14)   'I felt sensations of a peculiar and overpowering nature: they were a mixture of pain and pleasure, such as I had never before experienced, either from hunger or cold, warmth or food; and I withdrew from the window, unable to bear these emotions.' (p. 111)

Faced with the love and affection evident in the home of the de Laceys, the monster becomes painfully aware of the lack of any such love, affection and companionship for himself.

(15)   I saw at the open window a figure the most hideous and abhorred. A grin was on the face of the monster; he seemed to jeer, as with his fiendish finger he pointed towards the corpse of my wife. (p. 200)

The monster here shows the depth of his torment in genuine malignity.

Verbal ties

At a number of points in the novel Shelley uses verbal ties between the words of Frankenstein and the words of the monster. Through echoes such as the following between the creature and the creator, Shelley emphasises the extent to which the two characters are to be compared:

(1)   The monster says: '"Yet you, my creator, detest and spurn me, thy creature, to whom thou art bound by ties only dissoluble by the annihilation of one of us"' (p. 102). Compare this to Frankenstein's later observation: 'Never will I give up my search, until he or I perish' (p. 208).

(2)   The monster: '"I, like the archfiend, bore a hell within me"' (p. 138). Compare this to Frankenstein's: 'I was cursed by some devil, and carried about with me my eternal hell' (p. 207).

(3)   Shelley tellingly makes use of the word 'consummate' with regard to Frankenstein's wedding night — it is to be the night that the monster consummates his crime, as well as the night that Frankenstein and Elizabeth consummate their marriage. The doubling-up of meaning in the word lets the reader know that it will also be a night on which two further 'marriages' take place — the marriage of death between the monster and Elizabeth (a direct act of revenge mirroring Frankenstein's destruction of the monster's companion) and the marriage of Frankenstein and his monster in deadly pursuit.

(4)   Compare Frankenstein's: 'I would sell my life dearly, and not shrink from the conflict until my own life, or that of my adversary, was extinguished' (p. 198) to the monster's: '"you, my creator, detest and spurn me, thy creature, to whom thou art bound by ties only dissoluble by the annihilation of one of us"' (p. 102).

Shelley's use of this technique establishes in the mind of the reader an intimate connection between Frankenstein and his monster. Even though they are in many ways extremely isolated one from the other, Shelley uses verbal ties to emphasise the inescapable fact that, as creator and creature, the links between them are undeniable. Unconsciously they use the same words as one another. This may be seen to add weight to the concept of the doppelgänger in the context of their relationship.

The role of women

Women and Gothic

The connection between women and Gothic is an interesting one. Many of the foremost authors working in the Gothic genre have been women. Mary Shelley, the Brontë sisters, Ann Radcliffe, Charlotte Dacre and Sophia Lee were all early authors of Gothic and were profoundly influential in their impact on the development of the form and its concerns. Women certainly have a central role to play within the world of Gothic fiction, where they are frequently the victims of extreme male domination and cruelty. At the same time, however, the women of Gothic fiction, even where they fulfil the typical role of the victim, often demonstrate great resilience and strength of character, surviving through the hardest and harshest of circumstances. The fact that females were so often the authors of these tales causes the reader to consider exactly what the fascination of women writers was with the world of Gothic.

Mary Shelley was the daughter of radical parents, Mary Wollstonecraft and William Godwin — authors of *A Vindication of the Rights of Women* and *A Treatise on Social Justice* respectively. The reader would expect that the daughter of such parents would share something of their forthrightness in her treatment of social issues, including the presentation of women. *Frankenstein*, a novel that dwells largely in the masculine world of Frankenstein, the monster and Walton, deals extensively with the issues of oppression and demonstrates women (often strong women) living in the face of brutality and adversity. The reader needs to look closely at the women in the novel and consider how far they fulfil conventional expectations of the female and how far they divert from them.

Females in the novel

Margaret Saville

Margaret Saville appears only as Walton's correspondent. As such she is a receptacle, but not an active player in the novel; in this she may be said to fulfil something of the usual, passive role assigned to women in Gothic fiction. She is an outsider to the events of the novel, whose responses are not even presented to the reader. She holds in relation to Walton a similar position to that held by Elizabeth to

Frankenstein: she is cast in the light of the absent mother-figure who must remain at home awaiting news of the fate of her beloved.

Elizabeth Lavenza

Elizabeth, like Mrs Saville, spends much time in the novel waiting at home in Geneva for Frankenstein's correspondence. As he does with the rest of his family, Frankenstein leaves Elizabeth helpless in the face of his desertion. She is not, however, generally passive; she takes an active, if unfruitful, part in trying to save Justine Moritz when she is wrongly imprisoned for the murder of William. She is a strong character, coping with the repeated griefs inflicted on her by Frankenstein and the other events of her life. She is, however, cast in the light of Gothic female victim, both of the monster and of Frankenstein.

Frankenstein's mother

Frankenstein's mother is only present in memory in the novel. She is idealised, even deified in Frankenstein's mind as the perfection of womanly domestic virtue. His peculiar (deeply Freudian) view of her impinges significantly on his life, exercising a profound influence on his behaviour and decisions. A strong presence within the Frankenstein household, she leaves him with a lasting legacy, as when she (alongside Elizabeth) appears to the haunted Frankenstein in his midnight wanderings in the streets of Ingolstadt.

Safie

Safie is described as a woman of '"angelic beauty and expression"'; she is the object of Felix's delight and an image of perfection; her acceptance makes the rejection of the monster (the other outsider present near the de Laceys) all the more striking. Her background, like Shelley's own, incorporates radical elements: she is taught by her mother, contrary to Islamic norms of the time, '"to aspire to higher powers of intellect and an independence of spirit forbidden to the female followers of Mahomet"' (p. 127). In terms of the limits society imposes on her freedom, the reader may question whether her position is really very different from the Christian women in the novel. She has the courage to act on her own convictions, running away from and travelling independently of her father to rejoin Felix.

Justine Moritz

Justine Moritz is another strong woman in the novel who demonstrates great determination and moral strength in the face of extreme difficulties and injustice.

Agatha de Lacey

Agatha de Lacey is perhaps the most typically (or stereotypically) Gothic of all the female characters. Throughout the scenes in which she appears she is presented as innocent and weak, depending heavily on Felix to look after her, unlike the other women in the text who all demonstrate significant elements of independence.

The monster's companion

The monster's companion plays a highly significant role within the novel, even though she never actually comes into being. During her creation, Frankenstein reflects upon what the nature of the beast might be. Notice how he imagines the new monster to be a thinking, independent being, capable of making her own decisions and sticking by them in the face of the promises of the monster. She is envisaged as possessing strength and determination of character which may threaten and override the 'authority' of the male. Frankenstein fears this. Given that these imagined traits are characteristics a number of the other women in the text display, the reader is forced to consider the role such features play in the make-up of 'the female' and the issue of the male response to them. These are issues of considerable impact on the question of the presence of and the presentation of the idealised woman in Gothic.

Key passages and analysis

The following quotations all shed light on the novel's treatment of the image of the typical (or stereotypical) presentation of women in Frankenstein and in the Gothic novel in general.

(1)   ...when, on the morrow, she [Frankenstein's mother] presented Elizabeth to me as her promised gift, I, with childish seriousness, interpreted her words literally and looked upon Elizabeth as mine — mine to protect, love, and cherish. All praises bestowed on her I received as made to a possession of my own. (p. 37)

Notice here Frankenstein's view of Elizabeth as a possession (although the older, wiser Frankenstein recognises the immaturity and unreality of this view). She is presented to Frankenstein as some kind of trophy, as if she were a frail chattel in need of protection, love and cherishing. Given the evident weaknesses in Frankenstein's character, the reader quickly learns that Elizabeth cannot rely on her prospective husband for any of these things, but will have to rely on her own strength. Of interest here is also the role of Frankenstein's mother in the transaction. Such a marriage arrangement is a typical device within the world of Gothic fiction.

(2)   She [Elizabeth] indeed veiled her grief, and strove to act the comforter to us all. She looked steadily on life, and assumed its duties with courage and zeal. She devoted herself to those whom she had been taught to call her uncle and cousins. (p. 45)

Frankenstein talks of Elizabeth's selfless and self-sacrificing behaviour and role after the death of his mother, demonstrating great personal strength. Note the role of comforter (a term laden with biblical significance; the word is used in the New

Testament to refer to the Holy Spirit) that she adopts (and is expected to adopt) as one of her womanly 'duties'.

(3) My trifling occupations take up my time and amuse me, and I am rewarded for any exertions by seeing none but happy, kind faces around me. (p. 66)

Elizabeth's observations here highlight the specifically domestic role reserved for women at this time. There are clear implications of the woman's role as 'trifling' and it is also assumed that the domestic occupations alluded to are of sufficient interest to 'amuse' and 'reward' in their own right.

(4) We were soon joined by Elizabeth. Time had altered her since I last beheld her; it had endowed her with loveliness surpassing the beauty of her childish years. There was the same candour, the same vivacity, but it was allied to an expression more full of sensibility and intellect. (p. 81)

Elizabeth is presented here as the embodiment of female perfection. She closely resembles the typical, usually beautiful and intelligent heroine/victim of Gothic fiction.

(5) She was there, lifeless and inanimate, thrown across the bed, her head hanging down, and her pale and distorted features half covered by her hair. Every where I turn I see the same figure — her bloodless arms and relaxed form flung by the murderer on its bridal bier. (p. 199)

Here again Elizabeth appears as the typical Gothic female victim. Her lifeless form, draped almost artistically and curiously erotically across the bed, closely resembles similar scenes throughout the Gothic canon, but especially prefigures the victims of the other great beast of the popular Gothic myths, Count Dracula.

Shelley and the conventional Gothic woman

The reader needs to evaluate the extent to which Shelley's women can be seen as conventional Gothic figures. The women in the text all play significant and powerful roles. Even such seemingly peripheral figures as Justine Moritz, Safie and Mrs Saville force the reader to enter into a dialogue between the expected role and the actual role of women in the text. Shelley's presentation of them is far from straightforward or conventional.

The majority of her female characters draw on elements of the traditional Gothic female. However, all of them also display exceptional fortitude in the face of extreme pressure and difficulties. They are not the stereotypically 'weak' heroines and women of Gothic romance, as in the works of Ann Radcliffe and others; nor, with the exception of the unusual threat to Elizabeth from Frankenstein via the monster, are they the sexual prey of autocratic, dominating males. Shelley's females are more subtle and complex than the norm. At the same time as acknowledging the conventions of the Gothic form, Shelley goes on to subvert those very conventions.

One of the most striking ways this is visible within the text is in the influence the female characters hold over the male characters. Women are a powerful driving force in the lives of Frankenstein, Frankenstein's father, Felix de Lacey and the monster. All require and respect the role of women in their lives, although in the case of Frankenstein this is not without his early and tainted perception of Elizabeth as a possession. The women 'behind' the men we see employ restraint and demonstrate wisdom and power all too often unmatched by the males they support. Shelley's representation of males and females therefore moves towards an equalisation of the genders, recognising the need for balance.

This sense of balance is also evident in the novel's presentation of violence and victimisation. Gothic frequently insists on the threatening and victimisation of the female and much more rarely the male. The threat to females within the course of the novel is very clear, but it is not disproportionate when compared to the threats and victimisation that face the male characters. Females are victims within the course of the text, but no more so than males. Clerval, William, Frankenstein's father and Frankenstein himself all fall victim to the monster. As with so many areas in this complex and fascinating novel, Shelley demonstrates that the Gothic and its conventions cannot contain her tale and its messages.

Outsiders

The outsider is a classic figure of Gothic fiction. Representing the threat of the unknown, the unacceptable, the damned, the fearsome and the horrific, mythical figures such as the Wandering Jew, the vampire and Frankenstein's monster itself have become central not only to the literary tradition, but also to popular tradition. Shelley uses the convention of the outsider in the novel to considerable and subtle effect. It is essential to consider a range of ways in which she uses the device and to think about the reasons for this and its impact on the reader.

All of the significant characters in the novel are presented as outsiders in the course of events. As with so many issues within *Frankenstein*, Shelley's presentation of this is not straightforward. The reader often entertains a mixed perception of the characters in question, holding a variety of feelings towards them, according to whether they pose a threat to the society within which they live, are threatened by it, or both. To be an outsider is the norm in this novel. Shelley's tale is one of disenfranchisement, disempowerment, loss of identity, loss of cohesion, loss of relationships and the destruction of familial and societal ties.

Frankenstein

Throughout the novel, Frankenstein is an outsider, isolated in his own family, then at the university, and finally in the length and breadth of the world. To a considerable extent, his position in each of these cases can be seen as his own fault. Growing up in the bosom of a loving, caring and protective (possibly over-protective) family, his choice to isolate himself from it is both surprising and ominous. The contrast between his domestic security early in life and the extreme isolation of his later life serves to heighten the tragedy of his position (and ultimate downfall) for the reader. Finally, forced by the monster to the ultimate life of the outsider, he is left chasing backwards and forwards across Europe, with no security and no hope of refuge. He is an outsider within the natural world, separated from the beauty of godly creation by the ugliness of his own all too human choices; he is an outsider separated from his creator by means of his own presumptuous desires and consequent rebellion. In transgressing the conventional and acceptable bounds of human and scientific research, Frankenstein ushers in a life of isolation both psychologically (he cannot talk about his situation for fear of how others will react) and literally.

The monster

Like Frankenstein, the monster is an outsider in many ways. Human society will not accommodate him because of his looks; unable to see past the hideousness of his exterior, they reject him on the assumption that his character is reflected in his features. His position as an outsider is all the more tragically confirmed in the rejection of his creator, who not only refuses to acknowledge and care for him, but also cruelly fails to supply him with a companion. His life in the hovel next to the de Laceys, from where he looks on longingly at their way of life and the love they have for each other from the outside, exemplifies in pathetic fashion the desperation of the monster to fit into the world around him. He is isolated from his creator and from the rest of creation by the absolute will of Frankenstein, and is therefore condemned to a life outside the bounds of society. Realising that the conventional happiness of human existence and companionship are not to be his, the monster offers to live voluntarily as an outsider in the wilds of South America if Frankenstein will create him a mate, but is further isolated when Frankenstein destroys the companion he has been creating for the monster.

Safie's father

Safie's father becomes an outcast in Parisian society, where he has lived and worked for some time, simply because he is a foreigner. He goes on to alienate himself from his own daughter by his ungrateful and churlish betrayal of the de Laceys.

Safie

Safie is isolated with her father in being an outcast in Parisian society. Safie's position as a Muslim woman is also identified by Shelley; her lack of rights, as a female, make her position even within her native society effectively that of an outsider. When her father, with treacherous ingratitude, betrays the de Laceys, she

finds herself separated from her own flesh and blood, preferring to risk all in the attempt to find Felix.

Walton

Walton is isolated from his family and from the security of home by his geographical location. Like Frankenstein, he is a self-imposed outsider as a result of his burning scientific desires. Even on board ship he is isolated amongst the crew by his position as captain and by his desire to press on towards the pole, even in the face of the most extreme danger. He recognises the fact that he is to all intents and purposes an outsider from society and seems aware of the dangers he faces directly as a result of his lack of a good companion who could keep him and his ideas within reasonable bounds.

Clerval

Clerval is one of the nearest and dearest of Frankenstein's friends. He becomes marginalised in the affections of Frankenstein during the creation of the monster and is again distanced from him, in spite of his great loyalty to his friend, on their trip to England when Frankenstein is creating the monster's mate. In his desire to pursue his studies at university, Clerval's wishes are opposed to those of his father. Unlike Frankenstein, however, Clerval remains at home, resolves the difficulty, and does not alienate himself from those he loves.

Mrs Saville (Walton's sister)

Mrs Saville is an outsider who is given no voice. She is simply the intended recipient of Walton's strange correspondence, the final letter of which cannot even reach her unless Walton safely returns to port. It is a correspondence which, given Walton's geographical location, can only be one-sided, and as such is scarcely a correspondence at all. As Walton is the singular audience of Frankenstein's tale, so Mrs Saville is the singular audience of her brother's.

Elizabeth Lavenza

As an orphan adopted by the kindly Frankensteins, Elizabeth is an archetypal outsider figure. Having gained the love and acceptance of the family, however, she finds herself increasingly an outsider in Frankenstein's affections as a result of his scientific explorations. The acceptance she, like Justine Moritz, finds in the Frankenstein household, serves as a stark contrast to the bitter lack of acceptance Frankenstein shows to the monster later in the novel.

Frankenstein's father

Frankenstein's father is left isolated and lonely after the death of his wife, an experience which changes him profoundly. This is further aggravated by the way his son increasingly shuts him out of his confidence once he has left to pursue his studies at Ingolstadt. As his family members are killed one by one at the hands of the monster (a fact of which he is never aware), his position as an outsider becomes increasingly acute until at last he pines away.

Justine Moritz

Like Elizabeth, Justine is orphaned and taken in by the Frankensteins. She becomes an outsider to society (although she never loses the faith of her adoptive family) when charged with the murder of William.

The de Laceys

The de Laceys become outsiders in Paris, losing both their social position and their wealth owing to their courageous support of Safie's father in the face of popular prejudice. They become outsiders owing to the treachery of Safie's father. As a direct result of this they are forced to flee France and to live a humble and lonely life in Switzerland, a position exacerbated by their poverty.

Themes

Frankenstein is rich in thematic concerns. Think in detail about each of the following key themes, considering how they operate within the text, both independently of and in relation to one another.

Dreams

Dreams play an important part within the novel. Shelley makes use of the double meaning of the word 'dreams' in the course of her novel, i.e. dreams in the sense of a character's fondest hopes and dreams in the sense of sleeping visions.

Part of the effect of this is to point out the terrible irony of the destruction of Frankenstein's world of dreams; the world of his sleeping and waking dreams impinge upon each other — in trying to live out his dream he creates for himself a living nightmare. The use of dreams is a typical device within the realms of Gothic fiction. Gothic fiction deals with life at the borderlands of experience; as such, the world of dreams, at the borderlands of waking and sleeping, or the very edges of reality, is a perfect source of material. In *Frankenstein* Shelley makes disturbing use of the possibilities of dreams (for example, Frankenstein's dream immediately after the creation of the monster), operating within a well-established tradition employed extensively by other well-known authors of Gothic, such as Matthew 'Monk' Lewis and Edgar Allan Poe.

Here, in the immediate wake of the successful creation of the monster, Frankenstein's dreams descend into nightmare with frightening rapidity. Not only his scientific dreams, but also his perceptions of his domestic situation are affected. The contents of the dream encapsulate the whole of Frankenstein's story: the death of his mother, who may have prevented his foolishness had she survived, is graphically present, as is the coming death of Elizabeth. The dream is prescient of events to come, and incorporates the fascinating and deeply Freudian mingling of Elizabeth and mother in the dream (see pp. 92–94 for a fuller background on the significance of a Freudian reading of the novel). This dream represents a fundamental turning point; as Frankenstein goes on to observe to Walton: '…dreams that had been my food and pleasant rest for so long a space were now become a hell to me; and the change was so rapid, the overthrow so complete!' (pp. 59–60).

(5)   …I was overcome by the sensation of helplessness, so often felt in frightful dreams, when
         you in vain endeavour to fly from an impending danger, and was rooted to the spot.
         (Frankenstein, p. 172)

Essential to note here is the 'freezing' effect of nightmare. This is particularly significant in distinguishing the discrete roles of terror and horror within Gothic fiction. Ann Radcliffe, one of the first truly great authors of Gothic fiction, observed that: 'Terror and Horror are so far opposite, that the first expands the soul and awakens the faculties to a higher degree of life; the other contracts, freezes and nearly annihilates them.' Edmund Burke also discusses this issue, finding in terror an access to the sublime.

(6)   The whole series of my life appeared to me as a dream; I sometimes doubted if indeed
         it were all true, for it never presented itself to my mind with the force of reality.
         (Frankenstein, p. 182)

Shelley treads a very fine line throughout the novel between dreaming and waking, between fantasy and reality. Dreams emphasise the fantastic nature of the tale, but equally appear very real to the dreamer, operating right on the borderlands of fantasy and reality — this is where Shelley's tale, like so many Gothic tales, operates. Sigmund Freud, the founder of psychoanalysis, was convinced of the fundamental connection between the dreaming life and the real life of the individual, an area that he explored in detail in his book *The Interpretation of Dreams*. The concept is also of great importance in the work of Carl Jung, whose work, significantly for a study of *Frankenstein*, approaches the study of schizophrenia.

(7)   O blessed sleep! often, when most miserable, I sank to repose, and my dreams lulled me
         even to rapture. The spirits that guarded me had provided these moments, or rather hours,
         of happiness that I might retain strength to fulfil my pilgrimage. (Frankenstein, pp. 207–08)

The reader sees the comforting role of dreams for the now shattered Frankenstein. He protects himself mentally by a subconscious reversal of reality and dream. His dreams of domestic bliss now offer him his only means of escape from the horrors of a reality engendered by his initial grand dreams' creation. It is these dreams that sustain Frankenstein in his endless pursuit of the monster. These same dreams extend into a strange, delirious reality for Frankenstein, as Walton observes:

> Yet he enjoys one comfort, the offspring of solitude and delirium: he believes, that when in dreams he holds converse with his friends, and derives from that communion consolation for his miseries, or excitements to his vengeance, that they are not creations of his fancy, but the beings themselves who visit him from the regions of a remote world. (Walton, p. 213)

Sanity and insanity

On many occasions in the novel we are asked to question the sanity of what we have read, and the characters themselves frequently identify the importance of this idea too. This thematic area provides another example of the use authors of Gothic frequently make of contrast and opposition in their work. The questionable sanity of Frankenstein and Walton in their dreams and their frantic pursuit of them adds to the atmosphere of unpredictability and fear that Shelley wishes to create within the novel. As we have already seen, from the very outset of his tale Frankenstein alerts the reader to the element of the unbelievable (the questionably sane) within the story. This may be interpreted as providing an element of verisimilitude, or truth to life, in a tale which may otherwise appear entirely fantastic — if the reader sees the events as the 'creation' of a fevered mind, they become somehow more acceptable. The persistent presence of madness also serves to emphasise the madness of the enterprises that both Frankenstein and Walton are engaged upon. Many of the novel's threatening effects derive from this; the events are just close enough to reality that they maintain the ability to shock the reader.

Revenge

Frankenstein and the monster are locked in an endless cycle of vengeance. This becomes inevitable the instant Frankenstein refuses to recognise and care for his creature, a mistake which he repeats throughout the novel. Understandably, the monster wishes to avenge Frankenstein's lack of care and love, to which he rightly believes he is entitled; a responsible creator must accept the responsibility for his or her actions. Frankenstein's failure to do this leads to the total isolation and loneliness of the monster. As Satan does in both the biblical narrative of Genesis and in Milton's *Paradise Lost*, the monster seeks his revenge not by attacking the creator directly, but indirectly through attacking those most dear to him. The monster thus pursues his revenge on Frankenstein by removing love and companionship system-atically from Frankenstein's life — by killing all the members of his family. It is not only Frankenstein who rejects the monster, however, but all of mankind; even the kind and loving de Laceys cannot see beyond the hideousness of his appearance to the genuinely affectionate nature of the monster. Thus all humanity is seen to be guilty of the rejection of the monster, who correspondingly extends his feelings of vengeance to encompass all mankind. His deliberate implication of Justine Moritz in the murder of William Frankenstein is a case in point. This of course engenders a renewed determination for revenge in Frankenstein, whose initial wish to 'undo' his work in creating the monster resolves itself steadily into a determination to destroy his creation for the murders he has committed.

Exploration

Frankenstein is full of explorers and exploration. The scientific research undertaken by Frankenstein is a type of exploration; Walton is exploring the Arctic Circle; the novel is based in part on the exploratory science of men like Luigi Galvani; other explorers in the novel are Paracelsus, Albertus Magnus, M. Krempe and M. Waldman, along with all the other scientists in the university at Ingolstadt. Beyond this, however, the novel explores unknown tracts of the human experience and the dark recesses of the human mind and soul. Nearly a century before the work of Sigmund Freud and Carl Jung, Shelley's novel takes a voyage of exploration into the world of the divided self and the profound world of dreams, where sanity and insanity merge. The novel is also exploratory in that it broke new ground, taking the Gothic novel into new realms of genuine psychological depth, as well as paving the way for the genre of science fiction.

Imprisonment and confinement

Imprisonment and confinement are important themes within the novel. As events progress, Frankenstein finds himself increasingly imprisoned within his dreams and fantasies as they unravel themselves disturbingly into a nightmarish reality. As a direct consequence of his desire to find the secret of life, he finds himself trapped within a relationship with the monster and morally imprisoned by a set of responsibilities that he immorally proceeds to ignore. As the relationship with the monster deteriorates, both creator and creature find themselves prisoners within an inevitable, deadly and unbreakable cycle of revenge and hatred. Frankenstein is clearly a prisoner of his own imagination and is destined to live trapped within the workings of his own mind. He finds himself imprisoned literally in Ireland as the suspected murderer of his dearest friend Henry Clerval.

The monster, as a result of the rejection of his creator and the repeated prejudice he encounters at the hands of humans, finds himself trapped in isolation, revenge and hatred. His body, ironically created by Frankenstein to be beautiful, imprisons him in that it is the direct cause of his inability to establish relationships with those he encounters. The hovel next to the cottage of the de Laceys is an image of desperate confinement, all the more so given the monster's pathetic devotion to the family. The monster's rejection is universal, and as such the whole world is a prison to him.

Other characters, too, are imprisoned. Elizabeth is imprisoned in her relationship with Frankenstein. Their relationship is doomed to fruitlessness and death. Justine Moritz is gaoled for the murder of William, an act she did not commit. Safie and her father are incarcerated as aliens in Paris, the victims of racial discrimination. M. de Lacey is trapped in a world of darkness by his blindness, although ironically this ensures that he is actually the most friendly and liberated person the monster encounters. Beyond this, all humanity may be seen as imprisoned in a benighted ignorance, unable to see beyond the unpromising exterior of the monster and the fears that he engenders to see the genuinely loving and good nature this conceals and belies.

Life and death

This theme links to a wide range of issues in the novel. Shelley uses the story of the creation of the world from the book of Genesis extensively, and Frankenstein's dreams and desires as a scientist are all focused upon the discovery of the secret of creating life. In addition to this, there are the many deaths inflicted by the monster (and indirectly by Frankenstein). Frankenstein grotesquely visits and raids the charnel-houses of Ingolstadt to dismember the dead bodies for his experiments. Life is shown to be a kind of death for both the monster and Frankenstein. The monster uses imagery of life and death to indicate the inseparability of a creature from its creator, presenting Frankenstein with the stark reality that '[I am] thy creature, to whom thou art bound by ties only dissoluble by the annihilation of one of us' (p. 102). Almost like a marriage, the relationship is to last until death parts them. This thematic area also provides another example of the prevalent use of opposites and contrast in Gothic fiction.

Human/inhuman

This is a thematic area covered more fully in the 'Man and monster' section on pages 49–56. The issue of humanity and inhumanity, however, is central to any reading of *Frankenstein*. The reader needs to consider in detail the ways in which Shelley presents the behaviour of both the monster and the humans within the novel. Humans are frequently guilty of the greatest ingratitude and inhumanity, both towards the monster and towards other human beings, whilst the monster frequently demonstrates kindness, humility and the potential for love. Shelley's treatment of this issue causes the reader to question the extent to which humans are humane and how far they are, in fact, monstrous.

Loneliness and isolation

Loneliness and isolation are to be found everywhere in *Frankenstein*. All the major characters suffer from this. It is significant that Frankenstein isolates himself first from his family and then from his fellow researchers in the university, leading to his disastrous creation of the monster. On his voyage north, Walton finds himself lamenting his isolation and lack of a companion. The monster is separated from the possibility of ever engaging in society as a result of his horrific appearance. Henry Clerval is left by Frankenstein on their journey to Scotland, resulting in his death. Elizabeth suffers extended loneliness whilst Frankenstein is away on his travels and is left fatally isolated on their wedding night when Frankenstein, blinded by his own egotism (or wilful ignorance of the intentions of the monster), locks her in their room to protect her. Justine Moritz suffers in a lonely gaol for a crime she did not commit and suffers the threat of permanent separation from the church and from God at the hands of the bullying priest. Safie is isolated first in Paris and is then forced to travel alone, abandoning her faithless father. The de Laceys, too, suffer as social outcasts after they have been betrayed by Safie's father. Notice also Shelley's predilection for scenes of isolation and loneliness to reflect the pervasive loneliness and isolation of her characters; this serves to increase the reader's sense of danger, threat and helplessness.

Ambition and determination

Many characters in the novel show these characteristics in a range of ways, some of them laudable, some of them less so. Frankenstein and Walton are both ambitious and determined in the pursuit of their respective dreams; Frankenstein later shows the same dogged determination in pursuing the monster. The monster shows great determination in learning language, in simply surviving and in attempting to persuade Frankenstein to fulfil the responsibilities he has so shamefully neglected; when this repeatedly fails, he shows great determination in revenge. In the face of injustice, Justine Moritz remains determined and proud, as does Elizabeth Lavenza in attempting to clear her friend's name. Henry Clerval does not allow his desire to study to be deflected by his father's initial refusal, nor does he allow anything to stand in the way of his determination to be an unfailing friend to Frankenstein. The de Laceys and Safie also demonstrate great strength of character in the face of considerable pressures and hardships. Shelley's presentation of this theme requires the reader to consider the extent to which these characteristics are praiseworthy traits and the extent to which they are destructive.

Journeys

Frankenstein, his father, Walton, Elizabeth, Clerval, the monster, Safie, the de Laceys and others all undertake journeys, sometimes repeated and of considerable length. Indeed, in the later stages of the tale, Frankenstein and the monster are engaged in a perpetual journey. These journeys have both a literal and a symbolic importance. The physical journeys undertaken, often into rugged and inhospitable (and frequently foreign) terrain, reflect the psychological journeys the characters are involved in. Shelley's tale and the emphasis it places on the journey encourages the reader to see life itself as a journey.

Imagery

Throughout *Frankenstein* Shelley makes use of a variety of imagery, as outlined below.

Biblical images

The use of biblical imagery clearly links to one of the key source texts for the novel, *Paradise Lost*. The fuller implications of this are discussed in the section on *Paradise Lost* (pp. 22–29). Shelley's use of biblical imagery and language, however, plays an important role in its own right. First note the nature of the tale Shelley tells; ironically this is about both creation and apocalypse. The connections of her narrative to the story of creation are self-evident, but the reader also needs to note the implications of the events of the biblical story of the creation of humanity and its aftermath. The temptation and sin that lead to the fall of man can be seen as preparing the way for the later biblical narratives of the crucifixion, the resurrection and the second coming. Innate within the very account of creation, therefore, is the whole history of humanity; including the great events of the end of time, dealt with in the book of Revelation that concludes the Bible. The dark desires, the bestial nature of Frankenstein's monster as the book proceeds and the ravings of the half-insane Frankenstein himself all point the reader towards the monstrous and the bizarre, both highly significant elements in the concept of apocalypse. Similarly, in presenting the battle between good and evil, Shelley is dealing with themes close to the heart of the entire biblical narrative.

In addition, the tale can be seen as prophetic, a kind of wisdom literature. Whilst not being fully didactic in her approach to her subject, Shelley has clear moral intentions and offers the reader a set of strongly drawn moral messages. The words of the monster to his creator on the 'sea of ice' and elsewhere often carry the weight of the prophetic books of the Old Testament. The importance of this for the reader is great; the monster, like the Old Testament prophets, gives Frankenstein a set of stark warnings about how he should behave. He offers him alternatives, one of which will lead to the redemption of the stalemate that exists between them, while the other can only lead to death and destruction for one or both of them. Frankenstein ironically comes to see himself as humanity's only potential saviour, but in seeking to destroy the monster and to prevent the furtherance of his species by refusing to create a companion, he seals his own fate. Redemption and salvation, such central principles of the biblical message, have no place within the parameters of *Frankenstein*.

The elements

In a novel which deals with power and raw, elemental emotion, it is not surprising that Shelley makes extensive use of imagery of the elements. The power of the natural world is an apt representation of the characters and their shifting emotions, often appearing as an externalisation of those feelings and their potential, as when Frankenstein observes the morning after the death of his wife Elizabeth: 'The sun might shine, or the clouds might lower: but nothing could appear to me as it had done the day before' (p. 201).

Significant here is the notion of the four humours, where blood, phlegm, choler (anger) and melancholy (or black choler) are linked to the elements of earth, air, fire and water. The ideal temperament was believed to be one which contained all four of these 'humours' in balance, while the preponderance of any one of them led to an imbalance and a consequent failing in character. The use Shelley makes of the elements is therefore highly significant, especially in her deployment of elemental pathetic fallacy to create atmosphere. The most striking use of the elements occurs at moments in the novel where rationality and balance are least in evidence. Shelley uses the elements sometimes directly and sometimes ironically to achieve her impact on the reader.

As a significant part of the natural world, the elements are a central part of the nature that Frankenstein loves so deeply, and at times seem part of his punishment, 'to mock at my unhappiness' (Frankenstein, p. 76). The physical 'punishment' of cold and exposure on the 'sea of ice', for example, and the hardship of the elements on the Scottish isle, are like a form of divine retribution for his presumption and foolhardiness. The role of thunder and lightning storms in this respect is particularly important. Frankenstein's witnessing 'a most violent and terrible thunderstorm' (p. 42) begins a thread of elemental imagery which strikes to his very heart and to the heart of the novel as a whole. The power of the electric storm prepares the way for galvanism and the eventual vivifying of the monster; the awesome, destructive power of the storm represents the destructive power of Frankenstein's own desires, which will leave him like the blasted stump of a tree that concludes the storm.

Nature and landscape

Any discussion of the use Shelley makes of nature imagery and the natural world should be considered in the light of her extensive connections with the Romantic school. Her husband, Percy Bysshe Shelley, was a central figure in the Romantic movement, as was his close friend Lord Byron. Other significant figures within the movement were Thomas de Quincey, William Wordsworth and Samuel Taylor Coleridge, the latter two being cited in the course of the novel. Coleridge in particular, through his poem 'The Rime of the Ancient Mariner', exercised a profound influence (explored more fully on pp. 29–32).

Romanticism is notoriously difficult to define. The Romantic temperament itself defied the very impulse of definition, preferring to emphasise the indefinite and the boundless. With its preference for and reliance on the values of imaginative spontaneity, visionary originality, wonder and self-expression over balance, order, restraint, proportion and objectivity, the Romantics expressed a profound mistrust of the advances of the empirical science of their day. The natural world, with its abundance, wildness, creativity, even excess, was an apt symbol for these authors of everything that they admired and wished to promote. The influence of these ideas on the young Mary Shelley is both clear and profound. Frankenstein, the empirical scientist, in seeking to apply the rigid rules of his study fails in the act of creativity, producing an object not beautiful, but hideous.

The range of extreme and dangerous locations that Shelley employs in the course of the novel reflects the extreme and dangerous nature of her tale, and the perilous moral dilemmas facing the characters. Her use of extreme locations and landscapes also resonates with such key themes of the text as isolation, death and destruction. The locations frequently symbolise the inner turmoil and upheaval of the monster, Frankenstein and the other characters in the novel. They also provide a suitable backdrop to the extraordinary events her tale reveals. The polar region, for example, is at the very edge of human experience, as is Frankenstein's lurid tale of creation and destruction. He recognises this himself when he observes: "'Were we among the tamer scenes of nature, I might fear to encounter your unbelief, perhaps your ridicule; but many things will appear possible in these wild and mysterious regions, which would provoke the laughter of those unacquainted with the ever-varied powers of nature'" (p. 31).

The ambiguous role of nature in the novel is key to understanding the character of Frankenstein. It is with the image of a mountain stream that he introduces the tale of his downfall, and it is his inability to engage in a sensible, or 'natural', relationship with the natural world that leads to his inevitable destruction. His 'unnatural' passions blight forever his relations with and role within nature. At times he is 'elevated…from all littleness of feeling' (p. 99) and 'diverted' (p. 99) by the beauties of the world around him, at other times he is brought face to face with 'the awful and majestic in nature' (p. 100), and at others he is reduced near to death by the physical torment it can inflict.

Good and evil

The tale told by Walton, Frankenstein and the monster can be seen as an exploration of the battle of good and evil. It considers in detail the complex interaction of good and evil in the human soul. The concept of 'original sin' so central to the biblical narrative of *Paradise Lost* is at the very heart of *Frankenstein*. The novel questions how good can be turned into evil; the monster, initially a benevolent and loving creature, is transformed by his treatment at the hands of humanity into the ravening and vengeful beast of popular imagination. All of this adds to the important sense of the novel as a kind of morality tale.

In addition, the contrast of good and evil fits in with the Gothic's frequent use of opposites, exploring the potential of human science and human nature for both good and evil. The novel's focus on the terms of good and evil and their physical manifestations suggests the importance of the spiritual and recognises the existence of powers greater than man driving the world. The literary sources of the novel and the references Shelley makes to them also underline the supra-human powers at work in the world — the angelic realms of *Paradise Lost*, the supernatural incursions of 'The Rime of the Ancient Mariner' and the Greek deities of the Prometheus myth all emphasise this, clarifying the dangers inherent in the forbidden practices Frankenstein is indulging in.

Putrefaction and disease

Frankenstein's initial experiments take him into the grotesque and decaying environs of the graveyards and charnel-houses of Ingolstadt. His very life-work is intimately connected with the decaying and diseased cadavers he steals to conduct his experiments. It is ironic that his creation emanates directly from the putrefied bodies of the dead. The use of these concepts within the novel also carries great symbolic weight, however; the decay of the human body and its central role in the construction of the monster and of the novel as a whole can be taken to represent the decay of the soul and moral responsibility of Frankenstein. Likewise, it may reflect upon the decay of human society, which allows such explorations as Frankenstein undertakes and then thoughtlessly, even recklessly, rejects and refuses to care for their results. Moral and physical decay therefore operate together to symbolise the unpleasant and degraded nature of humanity.

Note too that Frankenstein, when rescued from the ice floes by Captain Walton, is consumptive and also suffering from a terminal illness. The exact nature of this is never established. His death is attributed to no named disease, but rather seems to spring directly from the cautionary tale he tells. Consumed by revenge and racking guilt, he descends, through his illness and death, into the very world of putrefaction and disease that he has inhabited spiritually and morally ever since he began dabbling in his scientific research.

Death and destruction

Shelley's images of death and destruction are closely linked to those of putrefaction and disease. From early in the novel, the reader is aware that Frankenstein cannot survive for long after his rescue from the drifting ice; he is suffering from a mortal illness. Death is constantly hanging over the events of the novel; one by one Frankenstein's family members die at the hands of the monster. It is ironic, however, that these deaths spring directly from Frankenstein's driving desire to create life (which he in turn ironically does out of death, building the monster's body from cadavers).

Again, the reader needs to be aware of the symbolic importance of these images. Through his thoughtless neglect of his creation, Frankenstein unleashes a dreadful threat on the world, a monster bent on avenging his rejection first upon his creator, then upon humanity at large. This emphasises the fragility of human existence. It is also important to note that moral death and destruction are reflected in the physical death and destruction that abound in the novel. Other important connections are made in the reader's mind between these images and the destruction of Frankenstein's hopes and dreams, as well as with the ensuing death and destruction of the monster's innocence. It is therefore entirely fitting that the novel should end with the deaths of both creator and creature, that of the latter symbolically at the North Pole.

The use of the contrast of the mortal and the immortal is also useful here. *Paradise Lost* and the Prometheus myth both examine closely the interaction of the mortal and the immortal worlds. Frankenstein, in seeking the immortal (he wishes to be remembered forever as a result of his scientific achievements), is brought crushingly face to face with the inescapable facts of his own mortality. He has sought to usurp the place of God, the immortal, and must suffer the consequences. Similarly, Prometheus transgresses the natural relationship between the gods and humanity and must suffer the punishment.

The supernatural

Frankenstein, the supernatural and the Gothic context

The supernatural appears in *Frankenstein* in a somewhat unusual way. While the story fits within the genre of Gothic, where the supernatural frequently has a role to play, and although the novel itself makes reference to the supernatural on many occasions, in a conventional sense of ghosts and spirits, the supernatural does not have any part to play. The monster is 'supernatural' in the sense that he is superhuman — bigger, stronger and in every way larger than his human counterparts. The whole horror and power of Shelley's tale, however, lies in Walton's (and the reader's) acceptance that the monster is flesh and blood.

In this, the novel diverts from the conventional supernatural to be found in novels such as *The Castle of Otranto*, *The Monk*, *Melmoth the Wanderer* and other great Gothic tales. Similarly, it does not adhere to the 'explained supernatural' technique favoured by Ann Radcliffe, where occurrences which have throughout the novel appeared to be supernatural are given a rational explanation at last. Shelley makes clear from the outset that this is no such tale — unless we accept the reality of the monster, the events of the novel, although incredible in their purport, lose much of their power to frighten and to warn.

At this point it is worth noting the power of restraint in Shelley's presentation of the monster. With the exception of Frankenstein's initially brief description of his creation, the text is surprisingly (and for many readers disappointingly) lacking in grotesque physical description and details. Here we need to remember the observations of commentators such as Sir Walter Scott, Ann Radcliffe and Edmund Burke, all of whom recognise the increase in fear to be achieved from the imperfectly perceived. In refusing to define the monster fully, Shelley allows her reader to paint in the rest of the picture and to create the thing that is for them the most horrible.

Elements of the Gothic supernatural are present in the reactions of the characters to the events that take place. For all that he is a creature of flesh and blood with, as he is frequently at pains to point out, genuine human emotions, the monster nonetheless evokes in all who see him reactions as if he were a ghost. As a stalking presence, following Frankenstein across the expanses of Europe, watching his every move, he shares many ghost-like qualities, and can be compared to other great wandering figures of the Gothic, such as the Wandering Jew and Count Dracula.

Other typically Gothic supernatural elements are imported into the text through the use of Coleridge's 'The Rime of the Ancient Mariner' as a source text — the poem depends heavily on the supernatural, and the aware reader will automatically provide supernatural colouring to the events of Shelley's novel. Milton's *Paradise Lost*, with its setting in the world of angels and devils, likewise imports a dimension of the supernatural to Shelley's tale.

Quotations and developments

Shelley's use of the supernatural is highly sophisticated. These elements within the tale impact upon the reader in a variety of ways. Often the reader is forced to question whether the novel's occurences are even supernatural at all. This begs the important question of how far Shelley wishes us to consider the events as natural, and to what extent as supernatural. Captain Walton observes:

> ...there is a love for the marvellous, a belief in the marvellous, intertwined in all my projects, which hurries me out of the common pathways of men, even to the wild sea and unvisited regions I am about to explore. (p. 22)

This observation early in the novel prepares the reader from the outset to expect the supernatural. As we grow in our understanding of Walton's character and desires, we see that this moment of self-definition encompasses not simply a credulity of the supernatural, but also a world-view profoundly tending towards the fantastic. Like Frankenstein, Walton's mind forever runs on the potential of his dreams. From the outset, however, the reader is forced to question what form the 'marvellous' will take in Walton's tale, and how it will affect him.

Frankenstein, in beginning to recount his history, warns Walton in the following terms:

> Prepare to hear of occurrences which are usually deemed marvellous. Were we among the tamer scenes of nature, I might fear to encounter your unbelief, perhaps your ridicule; but many things will appear possible in these wild and mysterious regions, which would provoke the laughter of those unacquainted with the ever-varied powers of nature... (p. 31)

From the beginning, Frankenstein identifies what appears to be the supernatural within his tale. He points to events that will defy belief and which under ordinary circumstances would appear incredible. The reader is, therefore, forced to question the nature of the tale that is about to unfold: are the events the creation of madness, genuinely supernatural, more than natural (preternatural) or simply beyond the usual pale of experience?

Speaking of his early studies in the field of the natural sciences, Frankenstein tells us: 'The raising of ghosts or devils was a promise liberally accorded by my favourite authors' (p. 42). This passage offers the first unequivocal reference to the supernatural in the novel. It alerts us to an essential element of Frankenstein's character — his ardent desire for experiences that reach beyond the normal (the paranormal). From early on in life, Frankenstein is actively seeking the supernatural through his reading of Paracelsus and Albertus Magnus. Ironically, he later fulfils these 'promises' when he rejects the monster, by whom he is haunted and to whom he frequently refers as diabolic. Frankenstein speaks of his upbringing:

> In my education my father had taken the greatest precautions that my mind should be impressed with no supernatural horrors. I do not ever remember to have trembled at a tale of superstition, or to have feared the apparition of a spirit. Darkness had no effect upon my fancy; and a churchyard was to me merely the receptacle of bodies deprived of life, which, from being the seat of beauty and strength, had become food for the worm. (p. 52)

This is an essential moment in preparing the reader for the role the supernatural is to play in the novel and in Frankenstein's life. Protected by his father from the supernatural in his youth, the adult Frankenstein is unprepared for the demands of adult life. His father's unwise censoring of his childhood reading and experience has left Frankenstein without a healthy understanding of fear and the realities of death, both of which can be directly seen in his subsequent experimentation and attitudes. Having been prevented from dealing in childhood with the issues and emotions lying behind ghosts and tales of horror, Frankenstein has lost the faculty of imagination (or fantasy), the world within which properly functioning adults frequently and safely work out the likely consequences of their actions and/or deflect them.

Speaking of the monster, Frankenstein says:

> I considered the being whom I had cast among mankind, and endowed with the will and power to effect purposes of horror, such as the deed which he had now done, nearly in the light of my own vampire, my own spirit let loose from the grave, and forced to destroy all that was dear to me. (p. 78)

Frankenstein significantly links the monster to a vampiric, supernatural presence. The comparison is telling, as the vampire feasts on the blood of its victims. The assertion of sexual power is also essential in the make-up of the vampire, as becomes clear when reading texts such as Bram Stoker's *Dracula* or Keats's *La Belle Dame Sans Merci*; this is an issue which clearly intrudes on *Frankenstein* through the triangular and sexually tense relationship between the monster, Frankenstein and Elizabeth Lavenza (which interestingly and directly compares to the similar triangular relationship in Stoker's novel between the Count, Jonathon Harker and his wife Mina). Significantly, Frankenstein here identifies that this vampire is 'my own spirit let loose from the grave', thereby recognising that the monster is linked to him spiritually, an essential part of himself. Again, this draws closely upon vampire legend, and *Dracula* in particular, which lays great stress on the spiritual intercourse that exists between the vampire and its victim/lover/host. A final issue of essential interest here is that, according to vampire lore, the vampire can only enter in and feast where he has been invited; in creating the monster, Frankenstein has invited it into his life and must now live with the bloody consequences.

On the remote Scottish isle where he has gone to complete the monster's companion, Frankenstein recounts:

> I walked about the isle like a restless spectre, separated from all it loved, and miserable in the separation. (p. 174)

This image serves to isolate Frankenstein from humanity even more completely than the location of the desolate Scottish isle has done; it suggests the living death he is experiencing as a result of his connection with the monster.

Referring to the magistrate in Geneva, after he has recounted the creation of the monster and its role in the murder of Elizabeth, Frankenstein says:

> He had heard my story with that half kind of belief that is given to a tale of spirits and supernatural events; but when he was called upon to act officially in consequence, the whole tide of his incredulity returned. (p. 203)

This serves to emphasise for the reader, who is thoroughly engaged in Frankenstein's narrative, the fundamentally unbelievable nature of the tale he is telling and to recapture something of the perspective of the outside world. The reader needs to question how far this is his/her own response to Frankenstein's tale.

Science, taboo and fiction

It is important to note that Shelley does not actually pass explicit moral judgement on the issues of science and research that she raises. She leaves her readers free to develop their own interpretations and views of Frankenstein and what he has done. Nowhere does she in so many words criticise or berate Frankenstein and the other scientists for the work they do. But implicit in her great tale of horror is a powerful moral warning of the potential dangers of unrestrained and thoughtless experimentation.

There is often a significant note of ambiguity in the way Shelley presents the issues of science and the attitudes of various scientists to their work. Frankenstein, for example, never repents the actual scientific research he has undertaken, he simply regrets the consequences of it; even at the last he cannot give Walton an unequivocal warning of science's dangers, looking to the possibility that another may succeed where he has failed. He sees science as a kind of disease with which he has been afflicted, or as some powerful narcotic which has made him as a drunken man, evidence of which he also sees in the character of Captain Walton. Walton's return to Archangel at the end of the novel is highly ambivalent — the reader is given no indication of the eventual fate of Walton and his crew, and whether he does see sense and alter his course (literally and metaphorically) in the light of Frankenstein's tale.

In the monster, the reader is given a grotesque symbol of the outcomes of irresponsible scientific experimentation. He stalks the pages of the novel like some gruesome laboratory animal, a composite and bastard creation made up of reconstructed cadavers. Like the grotesquely horrible hybrid beasts in H. G. Wells's novel *The Island of Dr Moreau*, the monster suggests the hideous underside of the human psyche and the potentially devastating outcome of careless scientific research. Shelley is at pains, through her presentation of both Walton and Frankenstein, to suggest that such research should not be carried out in isolation. The early emphasis placed on Walton's lack of a companion, and his almost immediate meeting with Frankenstein, points to the importance of minimising such dangers by working in a group, to allow for sensible checks and balances to be put in place.

While she clearly has reservations and is keen to give a salutary warning through her Gothic tale of excess, Shelley does not appear to be entirely opposed to the pursuit of science. The novel is not an anti-science tract, but rather an attempt to establish suitable boundaries.

Noble science

There are clear signs in the novel that the pursuit of science can be both noble and ennobling. The ability to explore and to analyse the world in which we live symbolises the power of the human intellect, and at its best it elevates for the individual and improves the mass of humanity. Both Frankenstein and Walton begin their explorations in the hope of benefiting the world. To the end, indeed, they maintain some vestige of the hope of using their discoveries to improve the lot of mankind. Frankenstein initially aspires to finding a way of preserving life, while Walton wishes to find a quicker and safer trading route than those currently used by sailors.

Destructive and dangerous science

While Shelley is never overtly critical of the practice of science, she is keenly alert to the many potential pitfalls and dangers it entails. By its very nature, scientific research is a field of study that seeks to extend the bounds of human knowledge. The scientist's desire to push at the boundaries of conventional understanding is risky; it leads to moral choices, which may or may not be made sensibly, and involves dangers, both literal and figurative. Walton and Frankenstein both operate, in their exploratory work, at the edges of human experience, where to operate effectively and responsibly requires the utmost self-knowledge, assurance and self-control. Both men, however, find themselves incapable of curtailing the impulses inspired by scientific research; they are easily swayed by arrogant desire and lack the wisdom to know when to stop. The anticipation and excitement of their work seem to act on them like a drug; Frankenstein uses these terms when he first hears of Walton's dreams of finding a polar passage: '"Unhappy man! Do you share my madness? Have you drunk also of the intoxicating draught?"' (p. 29). Walton, too, makes disturbing reference to the arrogant, driving desire of the scientist when he asks: 'What can stop the determined heart and resolved will of man?' (p. 24).

The key factor in the observations of both men is the inability to impose balance; under intoxication the body is literally incapable of maintaining balance, as under madness the balance of the brain is impaired. Likewise, determination and resolution, if unchecked by reason and responsibility, are dangerously unbalanced emotions.

The destructive impact of this is evident within the novel. The monster is clearly symbolic on a number of levels of the destructive potential of irresponsible science. Rejected immediately after his creation by an arrogant and unthinking creator, the monster is released on the world without a thought to his welfare and his future development. He is a bastard creation (an interesting later perspective on the ill-sorted fruits of scientific creation can be found in *The Island of Dr Moreau*), incapable of integrating into society by himself, and as such he develops into the scourge of his creator. The result for Frankenstein is that his view of the natural world is forever jaundiced; once a great lover of nature he finds himself, after the creation of the monster, incapable of maintaining an 'innocent' and uncomplicated relationship with the world and his own creator. Extending this, the reader becomes aware of the extent to which the monster symbolises the uncontrollable thirst for knowledge itself. He is the externalisation of Frankenstein's monstrous desires and the hideous potential of these passions. He is, in a sense, Frankenstein's double, an idea pursued in detail on pages 52–55.

Scientists in the novel

Frankenstein

From his teenage years Frankenstein displays a fascination with the natural world. He loves it so much that he wishes to understand the movements and impulses that lie behind the beauty he sees. This sparks his initial interest in the sciences, his first studies building in his mind a confusion of ideas from the natural sciences and the bizarre alchemical writings of Albertus Magnus and Paracelsus. Though they are rejected by his father, Frankenstein nevertheless continues to immerse himself in these authors and is successful in gaining a place to study at Ingolstadt. It is here, when he hears M. Waldman's lecture emphasising the elevated and powerful position of modern scientists, that his fascination and desire is fully captured. After this he becomes a highly proficient member of the university department, developing his knowledge and skills until he is able to pursue his studies in isolation. He gains the respect of his fellows in the university but, unable to check his desires, strays into dangerous areas of research, culminating in the creation of the monster. He offers his cautionary tale to Walton. The apparent message of the tale, however, becomes less clear when he ends his story with a highly ambiguous warning, reflecting on his own failure and destruction, but raising the possibility that others may succeed where he has failed.

Captain Walton

Like Frankenstein, Walton is a determined explorer. He is on fire with enthusiasm and desire for what he may find and achieve, and is apparently reckless of the consequences. The reader may doubt whether he truly comprehends the potential dangers he faces at all. He is drawn at once to the character of Frankenstein, recognising in him a man of very similar temperament and, in a different situation, a potential companion. He listens avidly to Frankenstein's cautionary tale outlining the dangers of unregulated scientific desire. His response, however, is ambiguous; while evidently moved by what he hears, and lamenting the tragic fate and destruction of the noble Frankenstein, he still retains, at least in part, the desire to press on with his journey at the end of the novel. It is only under duress, forced by the demands of his endangered crew, that he consents, somewhat grudgingly, to return to Archangel. We remain uncertain of the impact the tale has had upon him and of what he may do in the future.

it is this very inability to establish acceptable moral boundaries within which science should operate that leads to his fate. This links closely to the important concept of the edge and the extreme in Gothic texts.

Frankenstein has suffered through his contact with science, but the reader must question whether he has really learned his lesson. To the last, he holds out the possibility of another succeeding where he has failed and seeks to embroil Walton in his own life-work by begging him to pursue and destroy the monster.

Taboo: some key ideas

Shelley demonstrates that the human race is on the brink of the unknown, and questions the wisdom of pressing heedlessly into it for fear of the 'monsters' that may emerge. Shelley's use of Milton and the stories of Adam and Eve and Prometheus suggests the forbidden nature of the scientific discoveries Frankenstein pursues. Frankenstein yearns for the hidden and the arcane. Like Adam and Eve, he finds himself tempted to stretch after the forbidden. He wants to push on to enter the secret citadels of science.

The early pursuit of alchemy identifies the aspirations and determination of Frankenstein to push at the barriers in his pursuit of the secret of life. Alchemists searched for the Philosopher's Stone and the Elixir of Life, both supposedly sources of perpetuity, as well as seeking to turn base metal into gold. All of these things clearly attract Frankenstein, who seeks literally to find the source of life and hopes through his researches to ensure the perpetuity of his reputation and fame. He is not afraid of the consequences of his actions, seeing only the potential glory that may accrue to him. This offers a key insight into his later reckless scientific pursuits. Alchemy was, of course, by Shelley's time a discredited system of scientific thought. This in itself is suggestive, demonstrating to the reader the likely outcomes of Frankenstein's pursuits.

At the end of his life, narrating his tale to Walton, Frankenstein recognises something of the error of his ways and the impact the pursuit of the forbidden has had upon him. He observes to Walton:

> A human being in perfection ought always to preserve a calm and peaceful mind, and never to allow passion or a transitory desire to disturb his tranquillity. I do not think that the pursuit of knowledge is an exception to this rule. If the study to which you apply yourself has a tendency to weaken your affections, and to destroy your taste for those simple pleasures in which no alloy can possibly mix, then that study is certainly unlawful, that is to say, not befitting the human mind. (p. 56)

In a similar vein, he refers to the monster as 'the result of my curiosity and lawless devices' (p. 83). He recognises that he has transgressed — a key element of Gothic is the concept of transgressing acceptable boundaries — and that not only he, but he fears the whole world, may have to suffer.

The multiple narrative

Multiple narratives and Gothic

The use of multiple narrators is typical in Gothic fiction. Classic Gothic texts such as *The Monk* (Matthew Lewis), *Melmoth the Wanderer* (Charles Maturin) and *Dracula* (Bram Stoker) all make use of the device. It is used to considerable effect in *Frankenstein* too. The reader needs to consider why the author has chosen this method of presentation and the impact that it has. The recorded testimony of a number of witnesses could be seen to add plausibility to tales which otherwise may seem to lack verisimilitude (truth to life). In addition, it provides an interesting range of perceptions of a single event, enabling us to gain a more rounded view of what is happening, allowing us to see and empathise with the emotional responses of a variety of the characters involved.

The use of the device goes further than this, however. In *Frankenstein*, the narratives seem to grow organically from one another: it is impossible to extricate them one from the other, as they are so closely linked and interwoven — there is a real sense in which the narrative of the monster is a part of Frankenstein's narrative, as the two characters are related to each other so closely. Similarly, Frankenstein's narrative is subsumed within that of Walton.

The shape of the narrative

First consider the sequence of the narrative: Walton — Frankenstein — Monster — Frankenstein — Walton. Such a sequence can be perceived and interpreted in a number of ways; it might be seen as shaped like a 'V':

Walton				**Walton**
	Frankenstein		**Frankenstein**	
		Monster		

Such an interpretation would suggest that Walton's narrative is at the surface of the novel's events — it is the narrative 'present' with which the novel begins and ends. Below that surface lies the tale of Frankenstein — a tale bearing potentially destructive similarities to the future of Captain Walton. At the 'deepest' point of the tale lies the narrative of the monster, whose perspective embodies the deepest and darkest insights into the psychological world of the novel. The open 'V' suggests an open-ended conclusion to the tale. The reader is left uncertain at the end whether the monster has indeed gone to his death at the North Pole, and deeper uncertainties arise when considering Walton's eventual fate. Frankenstein's profoundly ambiguous closing observations on scientific exploration leave reasonable room for doubt in the mind of the reader as to whether Walton will or will not wisely abandon his voracious desire for knowledge and glory.

Another way of perceiving the narrative structure is as a set of Chinese boxes (or perhaps Russian dolls):

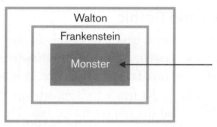

This interpretation implies a new set of relations between the narratives. Unlike the open-ended possibilities of the former interpretation, this view implies a closed ending to the novel. Walton's tale, the frame narrative of the novel (cast in the epistolary form inaugurated by authors such as Samuel Richardson and Tobias Smollett), encloses the narrative of Victor Frankenstein. The close parallels that exist between the two men suggest to the reader the close links between the two narratives, especially as we learn that Frankenstein's narrative is scribed by Walton and later edited by the teller of the tale. In view of the potential the reader quickly identifies for Walton to become another Frankenstein, the enclosure of Frankenstein's narrative within Walton's is deeply significant. Likewise, the narrative of the monster is enclosed within (we may even say embedded within) the narrative of Frankenstein. Again, this signals the inescapable ties between the two characters; as the creature of Frankenstein, the monster's narrative cannot be read as distinct from the narrative of Frankenstein himself. Nor can Frankenstein's tale exist without the overwhelming presence of the monster's tale. Tellingly, the monster's narrative lies at the heart of the tale — it is the 'heart of darkness', to borrow Conrad's famous phrase, of the novel, without which neither Frankenstein's nor Walton's narratives can stand. The concept of boxes is also significant in connection with Prometheus, who is sometimes linked to the mythical figure of Pandora, from whose box emerged untold horrors. The monster can be seen as being the 'box' at the heart of Shelley's tale, the box that Frankenstein foolishly opens, allowing the horror and turmoil of the monster's revenge to spill out into the world.

A third way of construing the narrative structure would be to view it as a set of concentric rings:

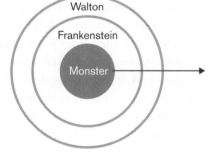

As in the previous construct, the monster's narrative is completely enclosed within Frankenstein's, which is enclosed in its turn within Walton's frame story. Again, this emphasises the inescapable interrelations and interactions between all three narratives. Such a view also recognises the overall enclosing structural possibilities of the tale. As with both the other interpretations offered here, this model points towards the middle of the novel as the deepest, central, most significant point — it is the monster that is at the heart of *Frankenstein*. The rings, however, suggest a different direction in the narrative. Whereas the 'V' implies a linear movement through the novel from Walton — Frankenstein — the monster — Frankenstein — Walton, and the boxes imply a movement inwards from Walton through Frankenstein to the monster at the heart of the novel, this model implies a movement outwards from the monster, driving all that the reader sees in the course of the novel. The narratives are like a set of spreading rings on the water of the reader's imagination, first perceptible at the circumference, but taking their impulse from the centre. Walton's first sighting of the monster comes before he has even met Frankenstein and therefore we see that the monster precedes Frankenstein in Walton's imagination; it is the monster that drives Frankenstein's insane pursuit and fuels his desire for revenge; and it is the 'monster' of scientific ambition in Frankenstein (a monster that also lurks in the heart of Walton) that leads to the sorry events we see.

Linking the narrators

Shelley goes to considerable lengths to link the accounts of her narrators. Through this she suggests significant connections between both the tellers and the tales they have to tell. These connections and parallels are explored extensively in the 'Characters and pairings' section on pp. 42–49. The detailed parallels between the lives of Walton, Frankenstein and the monster are emphasised continually by the tales they tell. Such is the impact of this that the reader soon comes to see their existences as integrally related. Indeed, in the case of the monster and his creator, Frankenstein, the distinctions between them become increasingly blurred for the reader until they can arguably be perceived as one.

The close linking of Frankenstein and Walton is also highly significant, as it emphasises the danger faced by Walton if he continues with his current course and does not alter his attitudes materially. The connection, via Frankenstein, of the monster and Walton must also be considered; the monster is at the heart of both Frankenstein and Walton, encouraging a range of symbolic readings of what the monster may actually represent. This encourages the reader to see Frankenstein and the monster (and possibly also Walton) as one and the same. Arguably, the reader may see in the three narrators Shelley's establishment of an unholy and alternative trinity: rather than the biblical trinity of God the Father, God the Son and God the Holy Ghost, the reader is presented with the father (Frankenstein), the son (Walton) and the unholy spirit (the monster).

Critical voices

Gothic literature is a form that has proved to be consistently difficult to define. It has manifested itself in many different places and at many different times. In order to gain a fuller understanding of the form, therefore, it is helpful to bear in mind a range of the critical contexts within which Gothic literature has been read. By targeting a number of critical points of view systematically, this section aims to provide a basis for thought and discussion when approaching any text within the Gothic tradition. This is particularly important given Assessment Objective 4, which requires students to 'articulate informed, independent judgements, showing under-standing of different interpretations of literary texts by different readers'.

The nature of Gothic

The archaic and pagan

> Gothic was the archaic, the pagan, that which was prior to, or resisted the establishment of civilised values and a well-regulated society. (David Punter, 1996)

Here David Punter suggests the essential historical connotations of the form; notice the emphasis placed on the importance of the past within Gothic. Typically, Gothic texts deal with a historical time past, for example *The Castle of Otranto* (Horace Walpole), *The Monk* (Matthew Lewis) and *The Mysteries of Udolpho* (Ann Radcliffe). Other texts, such as the modern Gothic tales *The Woman in Black* and *The Mist in the Mirror* by Susan Hill or *Gormenghast* by Mervyn Peake, are set in an indeter-minate time-world. A third group of texts, such as *Wuthering Heights*, *Frankenstein*, and Peter Ackroyd's *Hawksmoor*, veer between a narratorial present and related events from the past. Note too the emphasis upon the 'external' and subversive nature of the genre. Gothic, Punter suggests, lies at the very boundaries of the acceptable; hence it is linked with a historically remote time, or with the religiously suspect (witchcraft, the pagan, non-Protestant religion), the exotic and the foreign. Even where the action of the texts is established firmly in England, the location and action of the tales indicates the extent to which they represent values and demands that lie outside the bounds of the conventional and the acceptable. *Frankenstein* takes place in a wide variety of wild and dangerous settings and *Wuthering Heights* is set on the bleak and remote Yorkshire moors, while Susan Hill's *The Woman in Black* utilises the barren strangeness of the Eel Marsh to create its unholy and threat-ening atmosphere.

The bizarre and unfamiliar

> Gothic was chaotic...ornate and convoluted...excess and exaggeration, the product of the wild and uncivilised. (ibid.)

An essential element within Gothic is the uncontrollable and the excessive, the bizarre and unfamiliar. It is the continual presence of such elements within Gothic texts that creates the sense of the unpredictable and the disturbing, the atmosphere of threat and foreboding. The representation of violent and extreme action and emotion, often incompletely explained, and the use of wild locations creates a disturbing lack of security. The fictional world of *Frankenstein* makes considerable use of this.

The Gothic borderlands

Gothic works, it is often objected, are not fully achieved works: they are fragmentary, inconsistent, jagged…. If Gothic works 'do not come out right', this is because they deal in psychological areas which themselves do not come out right, they deal in those structures of the mind which are compounded with repression rather than with the purified material to which realism claims access…. And it is here that we come to the crux of the matter: Gothic writers work — consciously or unconsciously — on the fringe of the acceptable, for it is on this borderland that fear resides. In the best works, the two sides of the border are grafted onto each other… (ibid.)

This quotation identifies the importance of uncertainty and incompleteness within the world-view of the Gothic. The form represents its contents and concerns; the Gothic does not deal with the neat and the orderly, and therefore the works themselves are frequently neither neat nor orderly. Confusion as to action and motive are significant in that they indicate the very uncertainty and complexity with which the texts are seeking to engage. Frankenstein is a perfect example of this, proving peculiarly incapable of understanding his own desires and actions. His relations with the wider world, with his family and with the monster he creates are all problematic and illustrate the importance of confusion and uncertainty within the text. The growing complexity of the relationship between the monster and its creator (who may be taken as the opposite sides of the border referred to in the above quotation) is central to the text, and the distinctions between them become increasingly uncertain as the novel progresses.

Gothic and social upheaval

The rise of Gothic largely coincides with periods of political unrest and social uncertainty. The great initial period of Gothic coincides with the French Revolution (1789) and the anti-Catholic Gordon Riots (1780). Around the same period came the turmoil and separation of the American War of Independence. Throughout subsequent literary history, the appearance of Gothic has continued to reflect periods of instability (or the fear of instability). Mervyn Peake's *Gormenghast* trilogy, for example, was written in the shadow of the Second World War, and the tales of Sir Arthur Conan Doyle and H. G. Wells reflect the fear of the 'outsider' bred by the colonial system.

One of the most chilling fears that informs these stories is the threat of ancestral repetition. (Laura Kranzler, from *Introduction to Elizabeth Gaskell's Gothic Tales*, Penguin, 2000)

Frankenstein deals extensively not only with the possibility, but also with the reality of such generational repetition. Frankenstein fears the beginnings of a new race of monsters, and therefore disastrously destroys the companion he is creating for the monster. Similarly, the pattern of violent death is visited upon three generations of Frankenstein's family, and Walton, with his fascination for exploration, is a potential new Frankenstein.

Techniques of Gothic

Opposites and opposition

[The] juxtaposition of the ghastly and the everyday suggests one of the defining characteristics of the gothic genre, that of the uncanny double, the shadowy world that is the complex underbelly of familiar experience. (ibid.)

This quotation illustrates the importance of opposites and opposition in the Gothic. Here Kranzler suggests the essentially subversive nature of the form and its importance in providing an alternative perception of reality.

Blurring the edges

The Gothic was and remained the dimension of the imperfectly perceived. (David Punter, 1996)

Many Gothic narratives, including *Frankenstein*, gain considerable effect from blurring the edges of the narrative. Transitions from narrator to narrator and the varying perspectives they offer of events, along with the uncertainties engendered between the characters of the tale, who frequently parallel one another, are capable of creating in the reader the profound sense of insecurity and unease that underlies the form itself.

The forbidden and its attractions

It is in its concern with paranoia, with barbarism and with taboo that the vital effort of Gothic fiction resides: these are the aspects of the terrifying to which the Gothic constantly and hauntedly returns. (ibid.)

Here Punter highlights the essential role of the forbidden and its attraction within the Gothic. *Frankenstein*, like many other Gothic texts, deals with the forbidden and the dangers of pursuing it. This raises questions about the reader's morality and pleasure in reading and enjoying these texts.

Distortion and exaggeration

The Gothic is a distorting lens, a magnifying lens; but the shapes which we see through it have nonetheless a reality which cannot be apprehended in any other way. (ibid.)

Punter's emphasis here is on the importance of distortion and exaggeration in the Gothic. The larger-than-life and the twisted have a vital role to play, he suggests, in assisting the reader to approach certain less pleasant realities of life. In *Frankenstein*, the monster is in a literal sense both distorted in his physical repulsiveness and exaggerated in his size. His grotesqueness, however, reflects on Frankenstein's nature too, revealing the creator's character failings.

Gothic and religion

> These excluded areas...often retain a strong peripheral or inverted relationship with orthodox religion [and] embrace the practices usually termed occult. In such systems there is much more direct relationship with the invisible realms. (Clive Bloom, *Gothic Horror: A Reader's Guide from Poe to King and Beyond*, Macmillan, 1998)

Gothic fiction is notable for the frequent appearance of the devil and the devilish. The arcane and the forbidden is a staple element of the works of authors using the Gothic form, such as Aleister Crowley, Peter Ackroyd, Charlotte Dacre and Matthew 'Monk' Lewis. It also has a key role to play in *Frankenstein*; Shelley writes of a world where values are inverted, and where the presentation of religion is at best unorthodox. She makes direct and extensive use of the language of the devilish. The above quotation sheds an interesting light on the role of conventional religion in Gothic, a form which depends for much of its impact on a rejection of the orthodox and the establishment.

Realism and symbolism in Gothic

> Gothic fiction thus finds itself operating between two structural poles. On the one hand, because it rejects the account which realism gives of the world, it seeks to express truth through the use of other modes and genres — poetic prose, the recapture of tragedy, expressionistic writing, the revival of legend, the formation of quasi-myths — in order to demonstrate that the individual's involvement with the world is not merely linear but is composed of moments with resonances and depths which can only be captured through the disruptive power of extensive metaphor and symbolism. (David Punter, 1996)

Note the importance of symbolism as opposed to realism within Gothic. Shelley creates a fragile balance between them. The relationship between the two is essential — a preponderance of either element leads to an imbalance and a consequent reduction in the effect of the writing and its ability to instil fear and uncertainty.

Gothic and the supernatural

> ...the power of the older Gothic...is to use the supernatural as an image for real and carefully depicted social fears. (ibid.)

This viewpoint emphasises the social/sociological function of Gothic, as connected to reality. It suggests that the fear of social change and the socially suspect lies behind the use of the supernatural in Gothic fiction. The nebulous and indefinable nature of the ghosts and monsters of Gothic fiction and their predatory, threatening tendencies play on the social, religious and political fears of the reader.

Terror and horror

> Terror and Horror are so far opposite, that the first expands the soul and awakens the faculties to a higher degree of life; the other contracts, freezes and nearly annihilates them. I apprehend that neither Shakespeare nor Milton by their fictions, nor Mr Burke by his reasoning, anywhere looked to positive horror as a source of the sublime, though they all agree that terror is a very high one; and where lies the great difference between terror and horror, but in uncertainty and obscurity, that accompany the first, respecting the dreaded evil? (Ann Radcliffe, 'On the Supernatural in Poetry', 1816)

The difference between terror and horror is a key distinction as far as Radcliffe is concerned. She uses it to point to the morally elevating and uplifting potential of terror, as opposed to the morally and spiritually enervating impact of horror. Devendra Varma was one of the first critics to seize on this distinction, characterising the difference between terror and horror as the difference between 'awful apprehension and sickening realisation'. Robert Hume has also embraced this distinction, although in slightly different terms; he argues that the horror novel replaces the ambiguous physical details of the terror novel with a more disturbing set of moral and psychological ambiguities. Robert L. Platzner, while not challenging entirely the difference between terror and horror, notes where the edges blur. He refers specifically to the writings of Ann Radcliffe, but the application is more general: 'It appears that far from never crossing the boundary between terror and horror, Mrs Radcliffe compulsively places her heroine in situations of overwhelming anxiety in which a gradual shift from terror to horror is inescapable.'

Freud, Marx and feminism

Three of the most significant critical movements of the last century have been based on the writings and theories of Sigmund Freud, Karl Marx and feminist theorists. All three approaches cast an interesting light on a reading of *Frankenstein*.

Sigmund Freud (1856–1939)

Sigmund Freud, the psychoanalyst, formulated his theories in a series of books, *The Interpretation of Dreams* being the best known. His work led to many interesting developments in the literary world, including the rise of the psychoanalytic school of literary criticism, which has been highly influential. He is most famous for propounding the concept of the Oedipus complex (an innate sexual attraction to the parent of the opposite gender), the death wish, a focus upon the phallus as symbol and its corollary, penis envy, as well as the formulation of the divisions within the human psyche, which he termed 'id', 'ego' and 'superego'. His ideas and their appearance within Freudian literary criticism relate in detail to the fictional world of *Frankenstein*.

Childhood

Freud's concentration on infancy as the basis for subsequent psychological development is highly significant. The early portion of Shelley's novel focuses on the development of Frankenstein. Considerable significance is attached to the loving home environment within which he grows up and his father's notable failure to explain clearly to his son the reasons for his disapproval of the young Frankenstein's scientific research. Shelley also presents the reader, in Justine Moritz and Elizabeth Lavenza, with orphaned children. The monster is another significant example of this; Frankenstein, who stands *in loco parentis* to the monster, fails singularly in his parental duties of nurture and affection, leading to his passionate desire for revenge and the devastating events of the novel. Childhood is also significant through Shelley's portrayal of William, the first innocent victim of the monster, and the other children who, even in their innocence, reject the monster early in his life.

Sexuality

Freud believed that sexuality, repressed or otherwise, lies at the root of human behaviour. In *Frankenstein*, considerable emphasis is placed on the idea of 'consummation': Frankenstein speaks of the creation of the monster as the consummation of his dreams, tellingly avoiding sexual intercourse by creating rather than begetting a 'child'; later, fearing the results of a consummated relationship between the monster and any female companion he might create, he makes his fatal decision to renege on his promise to the monster. Frankenstein's marriage to Elizabeth remains strikingly unconsummated, the bizarre consummation of death between the monster and Elizabeth taking the place of marital sexual union. Shelley creates a significant sexual triangle between Frankenstein, the monster and Elizabeth.

Emphasis on the Oedipal relationship between parents and children is at the heart of Freud's theory and also relates significantly to *Frankenstein*. Shortly after he has succeeded in bringing his monster to life, Frankenstein has a nightmare in which the figures of his mother and Elizabeth become entwined. It is significant too that the marriage between Frankenstein and Elizabeth is hastened as the dearest wish of the dead mother, as if she and not the love of the two young people is the driving force in the relationship.

The self

The psychology of the divided self is a further crucial element in Freud's theory. He identifies a three-way division of the human psyche into the 'id' (appetite-driven desires), the 'ego' (conscious sense of 'self' and awareness of others) and the 'super-ego' (sense of morality, sometimes seen as conscience). In *Frankenstein*, Shelley fascinatingly pursues the development of the monster through various different stages, and Freud's divisions illuminate the reading of the creature's growth towards understanding and revenge. She also significantly presents the divided and deeply flawed nature of Frankenstein through use of the device of the doppelgänger; in this device, the reader can almost perceive an externalisation of the warring elements of the human mind.

The death wish

Freud saw the death wish as a powerful psychological drive, based on a continuing desire to return to the womb. This can be linked to Gothic's frequent use of dark, enclosed spaces. The garret where Frankenstein creates the monster, for example, is like a nightmarish womb. Frankenstein and the monster are locked in a pursuit to the death, and at times both express a wish that their sufferings could be ended by death (the monster's final desire is for self-destruction, and Frankenstein refers to his own death repeatedly).

Karl Marx (1818–83)

Karl Marx is best known for his great work *Das Kapital*, in which, with Friedrich Engels, he launched an outspoken attack on the capitalist system. His concept of 'historical materialism' has been highly influential in the Marxist school of literary criticism; this school seeks to understand literature as a form of material production that participates in and illuminates the processes of history.

There are many perceived social or political 'messages' within *Frankenstein*. The novel clearly poses questions with regard to the social implications of science; it also delivers forceful messages on social inclusion and exclusion and the potential consequences of this. The particular historical and sociological period of the writing of the novel can be linked to the key Marxist concept of class struggle. *Frankenstein*, first published in 1818, was written against the backdrop of European revolution; the monster can be seen as a symbol of the destructive forces of social and political revolution.

The reader also needs to consider how plot, characters and settings reflect the concept of class struggle, either by inclusion or omission. *Frankenstein* gives a symbolic status to both Frankenstein and the monster, allowing for a wide variety of readings in terms of the relationship between the powerful and the powerless. Shelley also makes extensive use of 'wilderness' settings, the harshness of which reflect the harshness of the monster's life and the brutality of the struggle between the creature and the creator. Shelley's use of a wide range of European locations serves to emphasise the universal nature of the dangers signalled within the novel.

A final key concept here is the way that, through class struggle, characters become 'outsider' figures and are alienated from society. The novel is full of such characters. Frankenstein and the monster both become social outcasts and misfits; similarly the de Laceys, Safie and her father are victims of society's rejection. Justine Moritz and Elizabeth Lavenza are also social 'misfits' in that both are orphans.

Feminism

Feminism is a modern tradition of literary criticism and polemic devoted to the defence of women's writing or of fictional characters against the condescension of a predominantly male literary establishment. Significantly, in the case of Mary Shelley, one of the earliest proponents of the feminist cause was Mary Wollstonecraft, her mother. A number of ideas central to the feminist point of view are highly relevant to *Frankenstein*.

The relative silence and passivity of female characters in Gothic texts has been noted by many critics. *Frankenstein* challenges many of the typical perceptions of women in Gothic; the women in the novel are no more helpless in the face of the monster than men; Frankenstein's mother, Elizabeth, Safie and Justine in particular are all notable for their strength of character. However, the stereotyping of female characters according to male fantasy is a criticism levelled at *Frankenstein*, in which Safie, Elizabeth and Agatha de Lacey are all presented as types of idealised female beauty and devotion.

The concerns and plight of women are dealt with in a number of ways. Frankenstein clearly perceives Elizabeth almost as a possession and as his by right. The text also highlights the position of women under Islam, through its presentation of Safie. Even though many of the women in the novel are strong characters, they are still largely obliged to live under the protection of males. As a text by a woman addressing the position of women in society, and women under threat, the novel explores the interesting relationship between the female author and her text, begging questions not only of male fantasy, but also of female fantasy. Given the importance of Freudian readings of Gothic texts, the reader also needs to consider the extent to which such issues could be seen as an expression of a female fantasy or wish-fulfilment.

Quotations

Look up the following quotations to find out who is talking and about whom or what. Select the most useful, i.e. the multi-purpose ones, and either learn them or make sure you could find them quickly in the exam. You may wish to add others of your own; keep them brief and consider how they could be used in exam essays or coursework.

p. 95   '...now misery has come home, and men appear to me as monsters thirsting for each other's blood.'

p. 96   'I feel as if I were walking on the edge of a precipice, towards which thousands are crowding, and endeavouring to plunge me into the abyss.'

p. 96   ...the fiend that lurked in my heart.

p. 102   'If you will comply with my conditions, I will leave them and you at peace; but if you refuse, I will glut the maw of death, until it be satiated with the blood of your remaining friends.'

p. 103   'I was benevolent and good; misery made me a fiend. Make me happy, and I shall again be virtuous.'

p. 103   'Yet it is in your power to recompense me, and deliver them from an evil which it only remains for you to make so great, that not only you and your family, but thousands of others, shall be swallowed up in the whirlwinds of its rage.'

p. 104   'On you it rests, whether I quit forever the neighbourhood of man and lead a harmless life, or become the scourge of your fellow creatures, and the author of your own speedy ruin.'

p. 104   For the first time, also, I felt what the duties of a creator towards his creature were, and that I ought to render him happy before I complained of his wickedness.

p. 122   'Was man, indeed, at once so powerful, so virtuous, and magnificent, yet so vicious and base? He appeared at one time a mere scion of the evil principle, and at another as all that can be conceived as noble and godlike.'

p. 136   'I am an unfortunate and deserted creature; I look around and I have no relation or friend upon earth.'

p. 140   '...feelings of revenge and hatred filled my bosom, and I did not strive to control them; but allowing myself to be borne away by the stream, I bent my mind towards injury and death.'

p. 143   '...I was not made for the enjoyment of pleasure.'

p. 150   'My vices are the children of a forced solitude that I abhor; and my virtues will necessarily arise when I live in communion with an equal.'

p. 158   '...he [the monster] had promised to follow me wherever I might go...'

p. 172   'Remember that I have power; you believe yourself miserable, but I can make you so wretched that the light of day will be hateful to you. You are my creator, but I am your master — obey!'

p. 189   How they would, each and all, abhor me, and hunt me from the world, did they know my unhallowed acts and the crimes which had their source in me!

p. 212   His soul is as hellish as his form, full of treachery and fiendlike malice.

p. 222   'Evil thenceforth became my good.'

Literary terms

The terms and concepts below have been selected for their relevance to writing about *Frankenstein*. It will aid argument and expression to become familiar with them and to use them in your essays.

allegory	extended metaphor conveying moral meaning
allusion	reference, either direct or indirect, to other texts
antithesis	contrast of ideas expressed by parallelism
black humour	humour that makes fun of something serious
caricature	grotesque exaggeration in portrayal of character
characterisation	the ways in which an author creates and develops a character
contextuality	historical, cultural, social, economic or political background of a text
didactic	adjective applied to a work of literature setting out to promote or teach a particular religious, political or philosophical point of view
epigraph	inscription at head of chapter or book
episodic	narrative divided into individual episodes
epistolary	taking the form of letters
first-person narrative	a story told from the 'I' point of view
genre	type or form of writing
imagery	the use of words to create pictorial images; often appeals to a variety of the senses — touch, taste, smell, sight, sound
irony	language intended to mean the opposite of the words actually employed; an amusing or cruel reversal of a situation
juxtaposition	placing ideas, characters or events side by side for contrast (often ironic) or to create other types of literary connection

myth	fiction about supernatural beings
narrative structure	the way in which a story is organised; may be chronological, reverse chronological, episodic, flashbacks etc.
omniscient narrator	a narrator who has God-like powers to see all events, actions, motivations and thoughts
parable	a story used to illuminate a moral lesson
pathetic fallacy	use of the weather or the landscape to reflect events, moods etc.
pathos	sad situation, evoking pity in the reader
personification	attribution of human qualities to objects, ideas etc.
plurality	possibility of multiple meanings of text
register	level of formality in expression
stereotype	a fixed type of character
symbolism	use of characters, actions and objects to represent higher, more abstract concepts
synopsis	summary of plot
third-person narrative	story told from the 'he/she/it' point of view
tragedy	a work of fiction that traces the downfall of a protagonist — often this character is initially seen as 'better' than the rest of us
unreliable narrator	a narrator the reader does not entirely feel able to trust (due to age, naïvety, self-delusion, tendency to lie, political reasons etc.)

Questions & Answers

AO3 excellent understanding and analysis of Shelley's use of language and how it contributes to meaning

AO4 evaluative, independent viewpoint; evaluation of others' interpretations; cogent argument about terror; engages with or challenges quotation

AO5i coherent linking of text and context in analytical discussion; excellent response to Gothic contexts and references drawn from throughout the text

2 Look again at Volume One, Chapter V of the novel, in which Frankenstein brings the creature to life. Then answer the following questions:

■ What do you learn of Frankenstein's attitude towards his creation in this chapter?

■ How does Shelley's use of language create the excitement and tension at the birth of the creature?

■ Many critics have commented on the importance of the birth motifs throughout the novel. What do you think is important about them?

Possible plan

Frankenstein's attitude

Frankenstein's initial tenderness and care before the monster is brought to life is followed by immediate disillusionment, as he realises how far from his dream the monster is. He is repulsed by the hideousness of what he has created. His nightmare demonstrates his fear and his sense that he has betrayed his family — in particular Elizabeth and the memory of his dead mother; this becomes inextricably linked with his hatred and fear of the monster. His reactions are of terror and horror: he sees it as devilish from the start — a 'demoniacal corpse'. He is disappointed with his creation and this leads to the early abandonment and isolation of it. He behaves wildly — this reaction reflects his inner turmoil. He fails in his duty as the monster's 'parent' — ironically reflected in the kind treatment Frankenstein receives from Clerval. He is driven to sickness and near to insanity.

Use of language

Shelley uses the language of darkness ('dreary night', 'half-extinguished light'); language of contrast (beauty/ugliness, dream/nightmare, hope/despair etc.); grotesque physical descriptions of monster; passionate language ('ardour that far exceeded moderation'); sudden, violent shifts of emotion; imagery of death. Note the juxtapositions of day and night, happiness and sadness, acceptance and rejection, friendship and hatred, urgency and lassitude. The pace of language creates immediacy and nervous tension. Note too the elevated style.

Birth motifs

In the previous chapter Frankenstein imagines himself as the beneficent 'father' of a new race of beings, gratefully receiving their thanks and adoration. This image of perfection is shattered quickly. His 'child' is hideous to him as soon as it becomes reality and he rejects it. The love and nurture Frankenstein received from his own parents (and others like Elizabeth and Clerval) reflects ironically on his own inability to display any love and care. The novel points out the duty of parents, a duty of care which Frankenstein fails to accept and apply. As a negligent 'parent', Frankenstein is responsible for the actions of his 'child'. The concept of the heavenly father could also be discussed, given the novel's dependence on the Bible and Milton.

Mark scheme

Grade C

AO2i some depth and understanding emerging on all three bullet points; sustained and developed sense of Frankenstein's attitude to his creation well illustrated by textual reference

AO3 understanding of how language contributes to meaning

AO4 states a view on the importance of birth motifs, beginning to engage with the critical view

AO5i appropriate connection of text and context; clearly explains the importance of Frankenstein in relation to ideas of creation

Grade A

AO2i secure, confident and well informed; excellent understanding of Frankenstein's attitude towards his creation

AO3 excellent understanding of how language contributes to meaning; conceptualised discussion of how this is used to influence the reader and to create tension

AO4 constructs a cogent argument about the importance of birth motifs, engaging with or challenging different views

AO5i coherent linking of text and context, conceptualising context of creation; excellent, wide-ranging use of reference

Examination essay titles

The titles that follow can be used for planning practice, full essay-writing practice, or both. They may be used as a basis for discussion or collaborative work, or on an individual basis for timed or extended writing. You should be aware of the need in all responses to refer closely to the text, supporting your arguments and comments with succinct and relevant evidence. Where appropriate, you may also choose to incorporate relevant critical material as a basis for your argument and response.

Whole-text questions

1   Explain how Mary Shelley uses the opening sequence of letters from Captain Walton to establish the themes of the novel. How do they influence the reader's view of the rest of the novel?

2   Discuss the ways in which Mary Shelley makes use of the device of 'the double' in *Frankenstein* and explain its significance.

3   '[The] juxtaposition of the ghastly and the everyday suggests one of the defining characteristics of the gothic genre, that of the uncanny double, the shadowy world that is the complex underbelly of familiar experience' (Laura Kranzler). Discuss with close reference to *Frankenstein*.

4   According to Ann Radcliffe, 'Terror and Horror are so far opposite, that the first expands the soul and awakens the faculties to a higher degree of life; the other contracts, freezes and nearly annihilates them'. How far do you find this a useful distinction in relation to *Frankenstein*?

5   Explain in detail what you consider to be the relationship between the interlocking narratives of Walton, Frankenstein and the monster. How does this relationship affect the reader's response to *Frankenstein*?

Passage-based questions: prescribed

Examiners advise that a substantial portion (up to 60%) of responses to passage-based questions should refer to the rest of the work being studied. Focus closely on the passage selected, but refer out from the passage to events which precede and follow it. It is essential to demonstrate how the passage operates within the wider context of the text as a whole. Establish the context of the passage and why it is a significant moment in the novel. Then go on to explore how it links to the rest of the novel in terms of character, plot, theme, technique and so on. Where a specified aspect of the passage, such as an author's use of language or imagery, is identified, ensure that this is a central element in your response.

1   Read again the passage 'I became acquainted with the science of anatomy… bestowing animation upon lifeless matter' (pp. 52–53). Comment in detail on Shelley's use of language and devices from the Gothic tradition and how this relates to the novel as a whole.

2   Remind yourself of the following section of the novel: 'No one can conceive the variety of feelings which bore me…correspondence as a proof that your other duties are equally neglected"' (pp. 55–56). How does Shelley's focus on the language of childbirth and family relationships in this passage relate to the wider concerns of the novel?

3   Look at the passage on pp. 97–98: 'I performed the first part of my journey…and blest the giver of oblivion.' Comment in detail on the use Shelley makes of contrasts in this section and relate this to the novel as a whole, explaining why you believe this to be so significant.

4 Refresh your memory of the passage: 'During this voyage we passed…the mountains of our own country'" (pp. 160–61). Comment in detail on how Shelley uses landscape here and in the rest of the novel to affect the reader and to create an atmosphere of impending doom.

5 Look closely at the passage: "'Alas! the strength I relied on is gone…I am only induced by reason and virtue'" (pp. 219–20). How far can this passage be seen as a reasonable and reliable summing up of the interrelationship of the man and the monster, and how, at the very end of the novel, does it affect the reader's views of both Frankenstein and his monster?

Passage-based questions: selected

When a task gives the option of selecting your own passages for specific reference, it is essential to select carefully. Failure to do so can lead to digression and even irrelevance. Ensure that the passages you choose are identified clearly for the reader and that they enable you to address the issues raised in the question specifically and in detail. Remember, the passages you recall and/or like best are not necessarily the most appropriate choices.

1 Choose two or three passages which focus on the monster. Show how Shelley uses these passages to develop the reader's understanding of the character and nature of Frankenstein's monster. What emotions does she encourage the reader to feel towards the creature, and how does she do this?

2 Select two episodes when Frankenstein and the monster meet. What do these episodes demonstrate about the relationship between Frankenstein and the monster? Focus particularly on the language of the two characters, their attitude towards one another and how these compare.

3 Choose two or three of the settings Shelley uses in the course of the novel. Explain in detail the reasons for her choice of these particular locations and how they relate specifically to the events of the novel.

4 With close reference to two or three episodes, discuss the ways in which Shelley makes the novel a criticism of the society of her time, commenting on the portrayal of women and the family, the use made of injustice, inhumanity and abuse of power, and the importance of money and position.

5 Select two or three episodes from the novel that deal with minor characters. Discuss Shelley's reasons for incorporating these episodes, discussing in detail their relationship with the wider concerns of the text and Shelley's narrative methods.

Sample essays

Below are two sample essays of different types. Both have been assessed as falling within the top band. You can judge them against the Assessment Objectives for this text for your exam board and decide on the mark you think each deserves and why. You will also be able to see ways in which each could be improved in terms of content, style and accuracy.

Sample essay 1

Consider Shelley's presentation of family and alienation in Frankenstein.

In the course of *Frankenstein*, Mary Shelley makes extensive use of the concepts of the family and of alienation. Typically of a Gothic novel, these two thematic areas present the reader with an essential opposition; the ideas of comfort, acceptance and unity naturally suggested by the image of the family contrast strongly with the loneliness and discomfort of the alienated being. These areas are dealt with in a number of ways in the course of the novel, but are perhaps present most clearly in the figures of Frankenstein and the monster. In the relationship between these two contrasting but inextricably linked characters, Shelley encapsulates the terribly ironic connection between these two themes.

The reader is first made aware of the themes of the family and isolation in the letters of Captain Walton to his sister, Mrs Saville. Through his own determination to succeed as a scientific explorer, Walton has chosen to separate himself from the rest of his family. Distanced from the home of his sister and the precepts he was taught as a young man, he finds himself in a far-off land and proceeds to isolate himself still further from his fellow men by undertaking a dangerous sea voyage in search of a northern passage in the Arctic Ocean. Through his letters, Shelley establishes at once the 'safety' of the family environment and the important protection it offers to the individual. Outside the family circle, Walton becomes deeply aware of the importance of companionship, both as a basic human need and as a means of regulating his behaviour. Shelley reinforces this message through the introduction of Frankenstein, whose life story is to provide a salutary warning, into Walton's world.

A deeply loved, maybe even a spoilt child, Frankenstein comes from a stable and caring home environment, but like Walton he has chosen to separate himself from it. His parents, siblings and adopted sister provide him with a youthful haven and an apparently ideal model of domestic happiness. Even from a young age, however, Frankenstein seeks to pursue his own course. Ironically, because of the very closeness and love of his immediate family circle and friends, he is made to suffer all the more as the novel progresses and he is forced to face the consequences of his self-imposed alienation. His move to the university of Ingolstadt isolates him geographically from his family and friends and also leads him further from the rest of humanity, from the reasonable bounds of human knowledge and ultimately from his creator.

It is ironic that as Frankenstein distances himself from his loved ones he seeks to replace them with a surrogate 'family' of his own creation. Shelley's use of imagery of parenthood and birth is significant in how the reader perceives Frankenstein's creation of the monster. In manufacturing a 'human' life form Frankenstein has effectively removed the need for human procreation and has divorced both himself and his creature from the conventional family unit and all the structures this implies. In so doing, Frankenstein fundamentally redefines the role of the 'parent' as well as the relationship within families between men and women. Shelley demonstrates this pointedly by presenting Frankenstein's laboratory or 'workshop of filthy creation' as a bizarre and disturbing alternative 'womb' as he works on his creation. He refers to his task as his 'labour', suggesting that he has somehow given birth to his creation, an impression reinforced by Shelley's initial presentation of the monster in terms that suggest its baby-like nature. In this context, the passing of time is also significant. Frankenstein informs Walton that 'Winter, spring. and summer passed away during my labours.' The length of the three seasons is approximately 9 months, representing the period of gestation for a human infant.

Frankenstein is driven forward in his research and ghastly work by the desire to become a father figure. He expresses the belief, prior to the final successful creation of the monster, that: 'A new species would bless me as its creator and source…. No father could claim the gratitude of his child so completely as I should deserve theirs.' He seems to want to create a race of beings which would be his 'children', and imagines an idyllic future of love and respect. The reader cannot, however, escape the desire for power and glory that also inspires Frankenstein in this vision of the future. It is a vision that proves elusive. Faced with the reality of his creation, which in life appears to him an ugly aberration, Frankenstein fails to accept the responsibilities of parenthood (which his own parents fulfilled for him), rejecting the monster immediately and leaving it to fend for itself. As he observes after the creation of the monster: '…now that I had finished, the beauty of the dream vanished, and breathless horror and disgust filled my heart.'

He refuses to accept the monster, and therefore does not love, teach or nurture it. In so doing he alienates the monster, starting a trend that is to mark its tragic existence from beginning to end. This same action also serves to alienate Frankenstein still further from his fellow men. He is starkly aware of how his actions separate him from the rest of humanity, creating a barrier between himself and them. Furthermore, in alienating the monster he makes for himself an intractable enemy who will, out of revenge, separate him from the family he so loves with cold-blooded determination, and who will ultimately hound him from the earth.

Such behaviour is not in the initial nature of the monster, however. A loving and intelligent being, it is only when faced with universal rejection and brutal isolation that the monster eventually descends into vengefulness. Frankenstein, in his ignorance, believes that this characteristic is innate, failing to see that it has only developed as a result of his own neglect of his creation. Because of his failure in his 'parental' duties, he has made the monster's delinquency inevitable, ensuring the descent of their 'family' unit into mutually destructive hatred and revenge, a cycle which, as the monster believes and observes to Frankenstein on the 'sea of ice', can only end with the death of one of them. Shelley's subtle combination of the themes of family and alienation, however, is such that the reader sees in this only a closer tightening of the bonds between creator and creature in their headlong career towards destruction.

The links between family and alienation within *Frankenstein* are evident. In spite of individual tendencies towards solitude and the desire for separation, Shelley demonstrates that alienation is neither desirable nor possible. The existence of the social unit, whether at the level of the family or at the level of wider human society, is essential for the main-tenance of healthy relationships and social stability, the only true freedom from this coming in the ultimate alienation of death.

Sample essay 2

Look at the passage on pp. 97–98 from 'I performed the first part of my journey…' to '…and blest the giver of oblivion'. Comment in detail on the use Shelley makes of the natural world in this section and relate this to the novel as a whole, explaining why you believe this to be so significant.

Throughout *Frankenstein*, Mary Shelley makes use of images drawn from the natural world. For her protagonist, Victor Frankenstein, such images are peculiarly significant. A lover of nature, as his numerous descriptions of it make clear, he finds himself increasingly divorced from the beauty of the world around him as a result of his own 'unnatural' reversal of the order of created life. The uneasy and tragic interplay between the natural and the unnatural in Frankenstein's character is identified early in the novel, when he tries to explain the course of his ill-fated life through the image of the mountain torrent and the recurring image of the blasted tree. It is also observed by Captain Walton when Frankenstein is first taken on board his ship in the Arctic: 'Even broken in spirit as he is, no one can feel more deeply than he does the beauties of nature. The starry sky, the sea, and every sight afforded by these wonderful regions, seems still to have the power of elevating his soul from the earth.' Even in the depths of despair and at the very end of his life, Frankenstein remains sensible to the wonders of the created order, an order that mocks and punishes him as his own 'creation', the monster, drives him further towards the extremities of existence.

These ideas are relevant to the passage under consideration here. As is so often the case in this novel, the reader is taken to a physically beautiful but also extreme location. This is a device often employed within the Gothic genre. Here, the wild and rugged scenery of the mountains, like the awesome and deadly beauty of the polar regions at the start of the novel, reflects Frankenstein's inner state. The journey he takes into the mountains, a place of danger and isolation, mirrors the scientific 'journey' of exploration and forbidden creation he has already entered upon and prefigures the personal 'journey' into tragedy and separation from his family that has only just begun with the deaths of his brother, William, and the innocent Justine Moritz.

Ironically, as he enters the mountains on this particular trip, which eventually leads to his confrontation with the monster on the 'sea of ice', Frankenstein feels 'the weight upon my spirit…sensibly lightened'. This demonstrates the power that scenes of nature hold over him. However, this is no Romantic ideal world. The beauty of the scenery and the strength evident within it speak to Frankenstein of 'a power mighty as Omnipotence', a concept which should fill the fallen and proud scientist with dread, but from which he strangely draws comfort. As he goes on to observe: 'I ceased to fear, or to bend before any being less almighty than that which had created and ruled the elements, here displayed in their most terrific guise.'

Rather than subduing the proud Frankenstein, the harshness of the location and the threat it poses to human life serve only to confirm him in his self-delusion. His use of vocabulary such as 'singular beauty', 'magnificent', 'astonishing' and 'majestic', along with his striking descriptions of the 'white and shining pyramids and domes' of the mountain scenery, demonstrate the extent to which he is moved, but also tragically underline the extent of his wilful blindness.

As he moves higher into the mountains, his spirits become elevated, almost to the point of trance when he enters the 'wonderful and sublime' valley of Chamounix. The use of the word 'sublime' here, echoing the 'sublime Alps' earlier in the passage, reminds the reader of the writings of Burke, who identifies the sublime, a state of heightened awareness and experience, as one of the most significant states of the human soul. The natural world, as so often in Romantic and Gothic texts, has this impact upon Frankenstein. The move into heightened experience and its comparative freedom from the troubling realities of life is reflected in Frankenstein's movement away from the rest of humanity. As he goes higher into the mountains, separating himself from his fellow men, so he is able to forget for a time the terrible realities of his life. Indeed, he is even able to relive, fleetingly, 'days gone by…associated with the light-hearted gaiety of boyhood', a condition of youthful innocence a lifetime away from the reality of his situation.

Such a removal from the overt realities of his life occurs as a result of the impact of nature upon his sensibilities. Shelley presents nature as a benevolent mother figure, an image laden with Freudian suggestions and tied closely to Frankenstein's idealistic and boyish memories of his own mother: 'The very winds whispered in soothing accents, and maternal nature bade me weep no more.' The almost narcotic power of such influences can remove Frankenstein from the pain and horror of his situation only temporarily, however. In a sense, the brief relief offered by his visions of nature serves only to torment him further, as he can no longer enjoy such visions with innocent eyes. The 'kindly influence' of the natural world soon wears off, leaving him once more in the depths of 'horror and despair'. Shelley emphasises the inescapability of his situation by her use of the word 'fettered', drawing attention to the mental and spiritual imprisonment that is now the reality of his existence.

Throughout this passage Shelley uses the natural world to draw her reader's attention to the terrible dilemma of Frankenstein's situation. His journey into the mountains emphasises both the heights and the depths of his character and serves to point out the irony of his position and the dreadful reality of the aftermath of his presumptuous creation of the monster. The stark contrasts of the mountain scenery, as well as linking the passage closely to the world of Gothic fiction and the concerns of the Romantics, externalise Frankenstein's inner turmoil and portray the dreadful dangers he now faces.

Using the critics

The role of literary criticism and literary theory in the study of literature at both AS and A2 is central. Assessment Objective 4 specifically requires students to 'articulate informed, independent judgements, showing understanding of different interpretations of literary texts by different readers'.

While this does not necessarily mean that all such interpretations should be by established literary critics or propound particular theoretical readings, the implication that these should be covered as part of advanced study is clear, especially where incisive and detailed analysis is required. Furthermore, the emphasis placed on a range of readings makes the use of criticism essential to success.

The following is an extract from the AQA specification, developing some of the implications of Assessment Objective 4:

Candidates will be expected to show awareness of the following:

- that, as readers, we are influenced by our own experiences, actual or imagined, and that our cultural background has an effect on our interpretation; thus the interpretation of literary texts, or the determination of their significance, can depend on the interpretative stance taken by the reader
- that there might be significant differences in the way literary texts are understood in different periods, and by different individuals or social groups
- that texts do not reflect an external and objective reality; instead they embody attitudes and values
- that there are different ways of looking at texts, based on particular approaches and theories. Using these theories will require some understanding of critical concepts and terminology
- that literary texts are frequently open-ended, so ambiguity and uncertainty are central to the reading of texts. Examination tasks will therefore expect candidates to take part in genuine critical enquiry rather than responding to tasks where the teacher/examiner already knows the 'right' answer

A wide selection of critical extracts, looking in detail at a range of issues innate within the study of the Gothic, can be found on pp. 88–95. This section contains a more extended and applied analysis of readings of *Frankenstein* from Marxist, Freudian and feminist critical standpoints too.

You need to think carefully about how critical material should be used. The emphasis in examination specifications is placed firmly upon a student's ability to recognise and evaluate the validity of interpretations from a multiplicity of viewpoints. Approaching a text from a single critical perspective, therefore, or prioritising one at the expense of others, is neither desirable nor helpful. Successful students apply and develop their critical thinking about the set text in the light of a variety of secondary critical texts.

It is essential, however, that you do not see the use of critical quotation as a virtue in its own right. Unthinking application of critical material is at best redundant and at worst prevents students from thinking for themselves. The key to successful application of literary criticism and literary theory is to use it as a basis for argument. There are three basic positions that can be adopted:

(1) To agree with a critical proposition and to use this to support an argument or part of an argument.

(2) To agree — with qualifications — with a proposition; identify clearly the areas of agreement, but go on to develop areas of disagreement, qualification, modification or extension of the ideas.

(3) To disagree with a proposition, explaining why.

All of these stances can be developed by going on to propose alternative critical or theoretical possibilities and evaluating the validity of one critical perspective over another in relation to the text or passage under consideration. To extend and enrich a response, the criticism used must be engaged with. Students need to identify the issues raised by the critic and then apply these in detail to the set text, which must always remain the primary focus of the response.

Further study

Wide reading is an essential ingredient in the success of the best candidates. A carefully selected reading of other texts by the authors you are studying, critical works relating to the set text and other texts written within the same genre is invaluable in helping you to understand the context of the text you are working on for examination. As you read, note features shared between the texts, explaining how this enlightens your reading of the set text.

The following list is intended to give a range of reading material within the Gothic genre. Not all are conventionally established Gothic texts; all, however, do draw upon the conventions of Gothic to a significant extent, or play with the reader's knowledge of Gothic conventions.

Fiction

Ackroyd, P. *Hawksmoor* (1986).
Austen, J. *Northanger Abbey* (1818).
Carter, A. *The Magic Toyshop* (1967).
Collins, W. *Basil* (1852), *No Name* (1852), *The Woman in White* (1860).
Dacre, C. *Zofloya, or The Moor* (1806).

Conan Doyle, Sir A. *The Hound of the Baskervilles* (1901), *Tales of Twilight and the Unseen* (1922).

le Fanu, S. *Uncle Silas* (1864), *The Wyvern Mystery* (1869).

Gaskell, E. *Gothic Tales* (first published as a collection in 2000).

Godwin, W. *Caleb Williams, or Things as They Are* (1794).

Hawthorne, N. *The Scarlet Letter* (1850).

Hill, S. *The Woman in Black* (1983), *The Mist in the Mirror* (1992).

James, H. *The Aspern Papers* (1888), *The Turn of the Screw* (1898).

James, M. R. *Collected Ghost Stories* (1931)

Lee, S. *The Recess, or a Tale of Other Times* (1785).

Lewis, M. *The Monk* (1796).

Machen, A. *The Great God Pan* (1913)

Maturin, C. *Melmoth the Wanderer* (1820).

Murdoch, I. *The Unicorn* (1963).

Peake, M. *The Gormenghast Trilogy* (1946–59).

Poe, E. A. *The Fall of the House of Usher* (1839), *The Black Cat* (1842), *The Pit and the Pendulum* (1842).

Radcliffe, A. *The Romance of the Forest* (1792), *The Mysteries of Udolpho* (1794), *The Italian* (1797).

Reeve, C. *The Old English Baron* (1778).

Shelley, M. *Valperga* (1823), *The Last Man* (1826), *Lodore* (1835), *Rambles in Germany and Italy* (1844).

Stoker, B. *Dracula* (1897).

Walpole, H. *The Castle of Otranto* (1764).

Wells, H. G. *The Island of Dr Moreau* (1896).

Wilde, O. *The Picture of Dorian Gray* (1891).

Poetry

William Blake *The Four Zoas* (1893).

Lord Byron *The Giaour* (1813).

John Keats *La Belle Dame sans Merci* (1819).

Edgar Allan Poe *The Raven* (1845).

Edward Young *The Complaint, or, Night-thoughts on Life, Death and Immortality* (1742).

Criticism

Gothic

Bloom, C. (ed.) (1998) *Gothic Horror: A Reader's Guide from Poe to King and Beyond*, Macmillan.

Davenport-Hines, R. (1998) *Gothic: Four Hundred Years of Excess, Horror, Evil and Ruin*, Fourth Estate.

Haggerty, G. *Gothic Fiction/Gothic Form*, Pennsylvania State University Press.

Hume, R. (1969) 'Gothic vs Romantic: a revaluation of the Gothic novel', *Publications of the Modern Languages Association*, LXXXIV.

Kilgour, M. (1995) *The Rise of the Gothic Novel*, Routledge.

Platzner, R. L. (1980) *The Metaphysical Novel in England: The Romantic Phase*, Arno Press.

Punter, D. (1996) *The Literature of Terror*, Longman.

Stevens, D. (2000) *The Gothic Tradition*, Cambridge University Press.

Frankenstein

Baldick, C. (1987) *In Frankenstein's Shadow: Myth, Monstrosity and Nineteenth-Century Writing*, Clarendon Press.

Gilbert, S. and Gubar, S. *The Madwoman in the Attic: The Woman Writer and the Nineteenth-Century Literary Imagination* (Yale University Press, 1979).

Hindle, M. (1994) *Mary Shelley's Frankenstein*, Penguin.

Levine, G. and Knoepfelmacher, V. C. (eds) (1982) *The Endurance of Frankenstein: Essays on Mary Shelley's Novel*, University of California Press.